Kickass Conservative!

How I escaped liberal feminism to
become a freedom-loving Trumplican—
and how you can, too

Joy Villa

#1 Billboard and Independent Rock Recording Artist
Pro-Life Conservative Activist, Actress, Vegan, Afro-Latina

www.joyvilla.com

PRAISE FOR
Joy Villa and *Kickass Conservative!*

"In *Kickass Conservative!* Joy Villa shows why she is an American heroine
fighting for conservative values in America, and how you can, too. I'm proud to
call her a friend. Her stories and experiences will illuminate the darkness
in today's political climate."

—DINESH D'SOUZA, filmmaker, author of *The United States of Socialism:
Who's Behind It. Why It's Evil. How to Stop It.*

"Joy Villa is one of the most courageous women I've ever met. She's a born
leader and a true friend. She inspired me to come out of the 'Trump closet'
and be myself, and for that, I am forever grateful."

—RICKY REBEL, Billboard Top 40 recording artist

"Joy's story highlights American values we should all hold dear: free speech
and free thought. In the face of a dangerous cancel culture that seeks to
suppress and silence, her message is timely and important."

—ORY RINAT, White House chief digital officer

"She's a beautiful warrior for all things good and true. In spite of
persecution and absurd consequences, Joy has boldly taken a stand for the
American principles our country was founded on: the pursuit of liberty
and justice for all."

—STACEY DASH, actress, co-chair, Women for Trump Advisory Board

"I am so excited for everyone to read *Kickass Conservative!* Not only is
Joy a talented artist and entertainer, she is an influencer and activist who
understands our current culture and the challenges we face as a nation. I
admire her boldness and determination to defend values that I, myself, hold
dear. I am confident this book will be yet another success in her sensational
and inspiring career."

—ABBY JOHNSON, Planned Parenthood director-turned-pro-life advocate

"Joy brings hope to life. A good read."

—ALVEDA KING, evangelist, civil rights activist

"In the increasingly dark world of the entertainment industry, Joy Villa is a light. It's so refreshing to see a woman so bold, brave, and unashamed. She embodies the term 'kickass conservative' and is a role model for all girls to stand out among the crowd, go against the grain, and use their voices to make real change."

—THE DEPLORABLE CHOIR (Cjaye and Lyndsey)

"I've known Joy for a while. Her passion and desire to make this country great is intoxicating. Her pure love for humanity is rich in true feelings and makes all those close to her feel better about themselves. Joy's attitude toward life is something everyone can learn from and emulate, and now it's captured in this book. Read and learn. Read and think. Read and know more about my friend Joy."

—WAYNE DUPREE, host, *The Wayne Dupree Show*

"Lucky me! I am honored to have had the fantastic experience of creating motion-picture art with my now-good friend Joy Villa. She plays the lead role of Maria in our feature film *The Contrast*, and she knocked it out of the park. Mark your calendars: We're looking forward to a release in January 2021. Of the many positive words to say about her book, and about Joy herself, I choose empowering and authentic. These capture her personality and the essence of her writing. Read this book! It is full of positive messages for your own personal growth in conservatism, delivered in practical, actionable tips."

—CHRIS JOHNSON, screenwriter, executive producer, *The Contrast*

"Joy is a brave woman who fearlessly stands up for her ideals. She's outspoken, courageous, and tells her story with both humility and determination."

—TRISH REGAN, award-winning journalist

"If there was ever a definition of a patriotic American, it's Joy Villa. In a world where people are easily offended or afraid to stand up for what they believe, Joy stands up for her beliefs with an in-your-face confidence. Her transition from a liberal feminist to a Trump-supporting conservative is an absolute must-read! I couldn't put this book down."

—AUBREY HUFF, host, *Off The Cuff*

"Joy Villa demonstrates how faith in God and sticking to your beliefs is the key to success. She is a brave woman in a very tumultuous time."

—SCOTT BAIO, actor, television director

"Joy Villa is a smart, witty, courageous woman with a message everyone needs to hear. She's a woman of the times, not afraid to speak her mind. I have no doubt this book will inspire and encourage you."

—DAVID J. HARRIS JR., author, entrepreneur

"Joy Villa is a bold and courageous voice in the American cultural and political conversation. She is not afraid to break the mold and stand up for her principles, despite public backlash that would terrify most people, especially in Hollywood. This is a testament to her strength of character."

—ZUBY UDEZUE, rapper, podcast host, author

"I consider Joy Villa one of my best friends and I'm very proud to know her. She is strong, tenacious, beautiful, and intelligent, and she does not back down to 'the mob' when she knows she is correct. She is a lioness and a ray of light. We are currently in very dark times in our country and culture. Joy is one of the very few willing to stand up and shine the light of truth when almost nobody else will, regardless of how she is persecuted or misrepresented to discredit her message. What a hero woman and role model for young women. *Damn!*"

—MARSHALL BECK, acclaimed heavy metal musician

"Joy Villa is one of the rare people who isn't afraid to wear her passions on her sleeve—or her Grammy outfits! Bursting onto the national scene through the authenticity of her voice, she lives her ideals as a bold conservative and isn't afraid to make friends or frenemies by engaging with the other side in the search for common ground and solutions."

—POLITICON

"Joy Villa is an electric personality who never ceases to disappoint as a statement maker. Unfettered and unafraid, she goes where few conservatives will. She is a voice for many who feel voiceless."

—OWEN SHROYER, *InfoWars*

"Joy Villa is a powerhouse with a strong, influential voice that is much needed by this generation. She is a leader who stands for what's right, moral, and commonsensical. She's not afraid to speak the truth and she does it succinctly and articulately with originality, while still having the ability to be respectful, full of life, and just so much fun. She truly embodies her name—*Joy!*"

—JESSICA BOSS, Boss Pictures, actress, producer

"As an America-loving, Trump-supporting drag queen, I have to confess: The real *queen* out there has always been, and always will be, Joy Villa. She's the original conservative diva who took risks that paved the way for others to courageously stand up for our country in creative ways."

—LADY MAGA USA, performer, activist

"Joy's book may go down as an historical reflection of a pivotal time in our country's history."

—LCDR JOHN DAVID CASTILLO, USN (RET.)

* * *

MORE ATTENTION FOR
Joy Villa

"Congratulations to Joy Villa on entering the wonderful world of politics. She has many fans!"

—PRESIDENT DONALD J. TRUMP

"Great to meet the talented and beautiful Joy Villa at the White House!"

—FIRST DAUGHTER IVANKA TRUMP

"[Joy] is the bravest. Wearing a Trump outfit to an awards show— that's like wearing a rib eye at the vegetarian convention!"

—TUCKER CARLSON, host, *Tucker Carlson Tonight*, Fox News

"Joy Villa is, at her very core, a performer. She has lived the creative process through and through in her lifelong journey of transformation."

—*THE EPOCH TIMES*

"It wouldn't be the Grammys without a pro-Trump fashion statement from Joy Villa."

—*VARIETY*

"[She] is determined to make that red carpet great again ... [She] really showed courage."

—MARIA BARTIROMO, anchor, *Mornings with Maria*, Fox Business, and *Sunday Morning Futures*, Fox News

"Joy Villa continues her streak of Donald Trump-inspired red carpet looks."

—*USA TODAY*

"It seems fitting that Joy Villa—the aspiring artist who turned heads in a 'Make America Great Again' dress on the Grammy Awards red carpet [in 2017]—[would make] her Billboard Top 200 debut on Presidents Day."

—*FORBES*

"This [her 2018 Grammys dress] might be the most pro-life dress the red carpet has ever seen."

—*THE DAILY CALLER*

"Joy Villa is just the first wave of the new conservative counterculture."

—*BREITBART*

"Viewers were treated to a surprise ... after singer-songwriter Joy Villa unveiled a dress emblazoned with [Trump's] campaign catchphrase 'Make America Great Again.'"

—*BBC NEWS*

"[She] made a clear pro-life statement at [the 2018] Grammy Awards ceremony in New York."

—*THE IRISH CATHOLIC*

"Conservative artist Joy Villa takes on [the] 'behemoth' social media companies."

—*SKY NEWS AUSTRALIA*

First edition

Library of Congress Control Number: 2020914050

ISBN: 978-1-7354143-0-0

ebook ISBN: 978-1-7354143-1-7

Printed in the United States of America

Joy Villa Productions, Inc.
Los Angeles, California
www.joyvilla.com

Photograph credits appear at the back of the book.

To God for blessing me with my beautiful talents
and obstinate attitude to keep going.

To my incredible and very human parents,
Mildred Angela Villa and Joseph Mario Villa. You instilled
in me the courage and fortitude to be myself in the face
of danger and animosity. I will never forget your
wonderful influence on my life.

To my dear friend Stefan Aarnio (1986-2020). An author, a leader,
a badass friend. You will be forever missed.

To President Donald J. Trump. You enabled me to
reignite my values and beliefs in this country, a place
that is free and worth fighting for.

To all American conservatives.
We are the new rock stars!

CONTENTS

FOREWORD
by Brandon Straka

www.walkawaycampaign.com

I met my dear friend Joy Villa in August of 2018. Like me, Joy is an artist, a creator, and a rebel. Also, like me, Joy is a former liberal who has placed truth and integrity over maintaining one's popularity merely by going along with the status quo.

To be a liberal in the oppressive climate of the left today is antithetical to art, creation, or rebellion. The left now demands conformity. It contemptuously attacks those who express individual thought, particularly if the person expressing the thought belongs to a minority group that the left has deemed one of its useful victim classes.

Joy Villa saw through the smokescreen of the left and made a decision to be her own person—an artist, a thought leader, and a culture icon. She says what she wants, sings what she wants, wears what she wants, and doesn't let the crowd set the rules by which she plays.

She is a modern conservative, a rebel.

And yes, she kicks ass!

Joy is on the front lines of a new breed of modern conservative and isn't afraid to own her glamour, her flirtatiousness, her charm, and her charisma. She pushes boundaries, owns her strength, and looks absolutely dynamite on the red carpet doing it all.

It isn't always easy to #WalkAway from the crowd and be an individual who fights for freedom and truth—all of which makes being an American just about the greatest thing on Earth. But I'm sure as hell glad to have a kindred spirit like Joy to walk beside on this journey.

To Joy Villa—and to kickass conservatives everywhere!

Wearing My Heart On My ... Dress

The Red-Carpet Moment That Started It All

"Be yourself. Everyone else is taken." —Oscar Wilde

MY PALMS BEGAN TO sweat under the hot flashes of the cameras. It was the evening of February 8, 2017, and I was in Los Angeles, about to step onto the red carpet of the Grammy Awards.

As millions of people watched on television, I sashayed, plastering on my signature "Hollywood smile" so as not to appear nervous. I thought of my big-screen heroines—Dorothy Dandridge, Marilyn Monroe, and Hedy Lamarr—to give me strength.

I knew that my luscious lashes, cat eyes, and ruby red lips had been done to perfection by my longtime makeup artist, Nichole Ray, so that gave me confidence, too.

I threw my head back, creating an air of carefree glamour.

What no one could see or fathom was the irregularity of my throbbing pulse and an uneasiness in my chest mounting with every step of my silver-studded Louboutin heels.

As I made my way onto the red carpet, the tight dress underneath my white cape hugged every inch of my generous curves.

I stopped at the first "X" on the carpet as the Recording Academy handlers beamed at me. They were admiring my elegant yet simple look of all white, set off by the sparkles of my diamond jewelry.

Dozens of frenzied photographers began to scream my name: "Joy! Joy! Look over here!"

Sure, it was just another day of walking the red carpet at the Grammys, as I had done since 2015 as a prominent voting member.

But this time, I'd had a heart change about what I would wear.

Instead of aiming for the shock value of "wildly sexy," I had decided to reveal something decidedly *more dangerous and taboo*.

I glowed and beamed, my Marilyn Monroe smile belying the thrashing of my heart against my chest.

"It's showtime!" I whispered to myself as I approached another "X" on the red carpet.

Unforgettable Counterculture Moment

I began to unbutton the fresh white cape that flowed elegantly over my shoulders. The gleaming white of my teeth and the large, white flower in my coiled, kinky curls completed the look.

There was no going back at this point.

No goin' back!

As I calmly, seductively dropped my outer garment to reveal the front of my mermaid-tail wiggle dress, a dress I had decided to wear only months before the show and had revealed to *no one* in my inner circle—not my publicist at the time, Rick Krusky, and not my then-husband, Thorsten von Overgaard, or my older brother, Ryjin—I will never forget the looks on the faces of all the cameramen, camerawomen, handlers, security, and

I shocked the world in 2017 with this amazing dress!

steely-eyed celebrities standing nearby. There, showcased on my dress, in unapologetically bold and American red, white, and blue—and spelled out in precious Swarovski crystals—was the pièce de résistance: the phrase "MAKE AMERICA GREAT AGAIN."

With a calm wink, I acknowledged each photographer and videographer as they all screamed and climbed over each other to grab full-body shots of me and the shocking message displayed on my dress.

It was delicious pandemonium!

Here was a strong, proud, Black, Italian, and Argentine woman with natural hair—*an Afro!*—colorful tattoos, a curvy and fit figure, and a shining smile that signaled glamour and intelligence touting a Trump gown in the heart of liberal Hollywood.

Unbelievable.

But the show wasn't over.

Not yet.

I approached the final "X" on the carpet as I had planned and practiced in the designer's studio, and took a deep breath as I turned around.

I wiggled what my mama gave me to unleash the rest of my message ...

That's right.

There, in large capital letters, on the bottom of my dress in the back, was the word "TRUMP" spelled out for all to see.

Trump on the Rump!

Frenzy of Fans

Almost instantly, with all of my sassy moves, I gained worldwide recognition and amassed millions of fans as an independent, underground recording artist who now publicly supported President Donald J. Trump.

My then-three-year-old album, "I Make The Static," jumped to No. 1 on the iTunes album sales chart for the U.S., and to No. 1 on Amazon's top

My mantra: Life is made to be lived. Be bold!

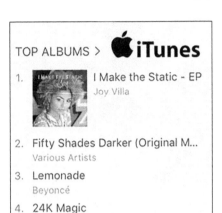

TOP ALBUMS > iTunes

1. I Make the Static - EP
   Joy Villa
2. Fifty Shades Darker (Original M...
   Various Artists
3. Lemonade
   Beyoncé
4. 24K Magic
   Bruno Mars
5. 25
   Adele

digital albums list. It also climbed up the top 100 of several other countries' iTunes charts, including Canada, the U.K., Australia, and Brazil.

In the next two days alone, my album sold over 15,000 copies. Also, practically overnight, my social media followings—to quote an article in *Forbes* about me at this time—"ballooned to reality-star level."

As that publication also noted, "Villa's Pro-Trump outfit immediately began trending on social media ... leading tens of thousands of Trump supporters to download the EP and flood iTunes' review portal with pro-Trump messages." Today I have well over 500,000 followers on multiple platforms, and the numbers continue to grow.

I also soon received thousands of letters, emails, and social media messages calling me disgusting racial slurs, vilifying my faith, disparaging my color, reproaching my body, bashing my political views, and threatening me and my family with death and physical harm.

It was the most exhilarating—and the scariest—few weeks of my entire career and life so far.

But this is only the beginning of my life-changing story.

I'm going to share much more about myself, both before and after that mind-blowing experience at the Grammys.

I'm telling stories in this book that I've never disclosed publicly before.

I'm sharing my honest take on what's been going on in our country.

I'm sharing my heartfelt beliefs with you and why I hold them.

I'm revealing how I stay healthy, motivated, and focused in the face of so much hate.

I'm telling you why I'm *a kickass conservative!*

And in the process, I hope that I help *you* find your own confident, kickass path as I did as a Trump-supporting conservative American who is unbelievably proud of this country—and who wants to do everything possible to make it better.

How to Use This Book

Here's the lowdown on making the most of *Kickass Conservative!* It's a fantastic how-to manual. Let me be your favorite big sister, your "MAGA Monroe"—as Alex Jones has called me—as I guide you through what it takes to be a strong conservative in today's social climate.

You can read it straight through, from start to finish. Or you can skip around and read sections out of order as they speak to you, as you need them in your navigation through heated political conversations with relatives and friends (*oh, what fuuuuuunnnnn!*), or as a comfort when things just get too damn lonely.

I've been there *soooo* many times. In fact, I'm still balancing my vulnerabilities and sensitivities as an artist who is introverted (I know, hard to believe) with my fire as a heroine (I hope!) for justice and liberty.

Some chapters may seem more crucial or electrifying to you at this moment in time, depending on your values, your interests, and your own conservative journey. Other chapters may inspire more reflection and inner contemplation. This is as much an action-oriented tome as it is a place to explore a true, inner heart change. It's a spiritual journey for me—and as a fellow spiritual being, no matter what your faith path may be, it's going to be a beautiful spiritual journey for you, too.

You'll also find practical tips at the end of each chapter to help you navigate your own path in the subject areas I cover. My advice: Make a point of checking them all out!

Since you're reading my book, I'm going to go ahead and tell you what will help you best: I ask that you read it once, twice, three times—then share it with others. Tell your friends about it, become a member of my JoyTribe (it's free; go to www.joyvilla.com to find out how), and live your most kickass conservative lifestyle!

As we look ahead to this year's critical election and beyond, I'm going to make sure you get as much food for thought as possible, especially if you're on the fence as you read this. Lukewarm is for lowlifes. Whether you choose to be hot or cold, read *Kickass Conservative!* with an open mind. Save those itchy Twitter fingers and really process what you're reading. There are also some goodies in the back of the book in the form of recommended reading for you as you take your conservative journey.

When everyone's against you—your family, friends, teachers, clergy, reporters, coworkers, bosses, and more—remember this: You have a trusty, good-looking bestie in me!

I'm going to help you prosper in America.

I'm going to help you be your best conservative self.

I'm going to help you succeed—and I'm rooting for you.

As you make your way on this journey, please reach out to me at www.joyvilla.com and let me know your thoughts, your experiences, your ideas, and your questions.

Whether you agree or disagree with me, I'm here for you. *Always.*

With Kickass Conservative Love,

CHAPTER 1

Using My Voice Over Violence: 2020 and Beyond

For Conservatism and Our Country

"Time to take real action, get a new reaction. Speak or move out the way." —Joy Villa, featuring Ricky Rebel, "Voice Over Violence"

B EFORE THIS YEAR OF 2020, few of us could have predicted the vast upheaval and unrest we'd be seeing across our country right now. I've been planning and writing this book—my first—for an incredible number of months. But as I've been putting the finishing touches on it in July of this year, there is still so much craziness going on.

And it may still be as you read this.

Our great, amazing, beautiful country is aching so badly right now.

It really took me a while—just like you, I am sure—to swallow the bitter pill that anarchy and a foul socialist agenda are now being enthusiastically embraced by the masses and proselytized by a weaponized media.

In the wake of George Floyd's killing on Memorial Day of this year and other terrible incidents, there's a rampant anti-police sentiment that has been ripping apart so many of our communities and cities, including the loud calls to defund and dismantle the police—which is not only completely ridiculous but dangerous. Who do we call when someone burglarizes our homes, Black Lives Matter? I think not.

There's the brutality of the recent rioting across the U.S.

There's the destruction of so many businesses, including the violence against *Black*-owned businesses, which is the antithesis of what this movement stands for, supposedly.

And then there are the stringent lockdowns and quarantines in our country because of the coronavirus pandemic this year, from which we're only beginning to emerge—*sort of!*—as I noted in an op-ed I wrote that was published on Wayne Dupree's site in June. (As I finalize my book, California has had over 466,000 coronavirus cases—that's out of a population of nearly 40 million people. Gov. "Gruesome Newsom" has been tightening restrictions once again. The state board of public health even banned singing and chanting in churches in early July. Unbelievable. What they rarely tell you is that overall deaths are down!)

In frustrating times such as these, I find myself occasionally feeling helpless. With my amazing platform of millions, I know I have a responsibility to speak out and use my voice against the violence that's been going on in our country. I reach out to God for comfort, grace, and guidance. My faith in the great Author of the Universe has given me not only the strength to carry on, but the strength to speak out.

Even though my own spirituality has shifted and changed as I've grown older, God has always been a big part of my life and always will.

Here is the truth.

I support Black lives. I support police lives.

These are sometimes the same thing.

Why the hell isn't anyone talking about this in the mainstream media?

Black Lives Do Matter

I'm extremely emotionally wounded by George Floyd's death on a Minneapolis street at the hands of horrible cops this year. No matter Floyd's past or what he was doing there that day, it was and will always be an unjust atrocity. On May 25, 2020, an officer named Derek Chauvin knelt on Floyd's neck for nearly nine minutes until he died.

Three other cops also applied pressure to Floyd's body during the dreadful, sickening incident. All four cops were fired and they're facing charges.

The viciousness against Floyd, who was 46, was captured on video, and it's become a flashpoint this year for vast social unrest.

We cannot have one more unarmed man killed by bad police officers in this country. One death like this is one too many.

But if all Black lives matter, which of course they do, *then what about the lives of our Black police officers?*

Nationally, over 15 percent of our law enforcement is Black, as many sources, including Axios, have reported. That's a bigger share than the overall Black population in the U.S.

These officers are doing a job that they get paid to do. They put their lives on the line every day to do it. I'm grateful for all of the great work by so many police officers, day in and day out, across our great country.

But look at what happened to David Dorn, the 77-year-old retired police captain. He served on the police force for 38 years. He was working as a security guard at a pawn shop when a looter shot him dead on June 2, 2020, during the crazy destruction and unrest in St. Louis, Missouri.

What about his Black life?

And look at what happened to federal security guard Dave Patrick Underwood, 53, who was brutally murdered on May 29, 2020, in a drive-by shooting during all the upset in downtown Oakland, California.

What about his Black life?

"Where is the outrage for a fallen officer that also happens to be African-American?" his own sister, Angela Underwood Jacobs, asked during her wrenching televised testimony on Capitol Hill in early June. I could barely watch that without crying.

And look at the insane abortion rate for Black women in the U.S., which is nearly five times that of White women, according to the Guttmacher Institute. African-Americans comprise just over 13 percent of our U.S. population—yet in 2014, Black women had 36 percent of all the abortions, according to Right to Life organizations. (The percentage may be even higher than that.)

In New York City alone, to name one location, thousands more Black babies are aborted every year than are born alive, as a *Wall Street Journal* op-ed noted not that long ago.

What about the lives of all the Black unborn babies in our country?

In today's overheated rhetoric, I don't hear much about those Black lives.

The truth is that we cannot pick and choose which humans matter to us merely to suit a socialist agenda that wants war over peace.

What's been happening in our country is tragic, heartbreaking, and wrong. The rhetoric and media-created narratives will not stand.

We have the right to speak up and speak out, and to do so peacefully. These are cherished First Amendment protections, as conservatives like myself know and hold dear. But the looting, the violence, and the destruction that we've seen after George Floyd's death can do nothing to bring him back.

And that was never, ever what his family wanted.

As an Afro-Latina, as a woman, as a recording artist, as an entertainer, as a writer—and most of all, as a freedom-loving American and a Trumplican—I am choosing to use my voice over violence.

I reject violence.

This book and my new song, "Voice Over Violence," are some of the ways I'm using my voice over violence. (Check out my new song on all music platforms and at www.joyvilla.com. And see the full lyrics to "Voice Over Violence" at the end of this chapter.)

But there's more!

That Hollywood and Highland Photo

In early June, in the middle of those turbulent and violent riots that took place at Hollywood and Highland in L.A., I walked out to that corner. I took an American flag with me, and I wrapped myself in that American flag as my photographer, Matthew Cali, snapped some pictures.

I wanted to show my love of this country. I wanted to make a bold statement amid the protests, the rioting, the looting, the destruction, and the chaos.

So much violence. It was sickening to me.

It still is. I am aghast at all that was destroyed and defaced and what's still going on at this moment.

As stores were smashed and voices were raised, I lifted my hand in peace. I waved at the National Guard troops who were there to help us. Once they acknowledged me and indicated that it was OK, I walked over to a group of them who were stationed there. I let them know that I supported them and that I appreciated how they were keeping us safe during these times.

I told them that I support both Black lives *and* police lives.

One gentleman in the group, who was Hispanic, told me that they had driven three hours to be at Hollywood and Highland and had not slept in 36 hours. When these members of the National Guard did get to sleep, they had to doze on the dirt-covered ground, the dirty floor—

with M-16s lying next to them for safety. They slept with one eye open.

They had families as well, they told me.

They understood the protests that were going on and the desire of many Americans to speak out, to share messages they so firmly believed.

But with all the criminal activity going on—the looting, the fires, and so much more—the goal of the Guard was to keep everyone safe.

This happened in the heart of the once-glamorous city that I call home. In many other cities and states, the same thing was happening as well.

Instead of all that destruction, I've chosen to use my voice over violence during these times—to speak, not destroy. To create, not desecrate. To be positive, not negative. And I've said this on the many media outlets that have reached out to me over these past months.

Prompted by everything that's been going on and determined to remain productive—and maybe even kick it up a notch!—I went into the stu-

Me, in L.A., in early June 2020. The National Guard troops were there to keep us safe.

dio to record my thoughts in musical form, to stand up for what I believe, and to do my part to help heal this nation.

My new song, "Voice Over Violence," is the result.

Ricky Rebel, an incredible pop artist, lends his phenomenal talents (he was discovered by Michael Jackson and signed to Madonna's label, and he toured with Britney Spears). We've been friends since 2015 and were drawn to each other as artists. We both have a message of love and empowerment. We're both conservatives. He came out for Trump after I urged him to, knowing he felt trapped yet again; but beyond his brave decision to come out as a proud LGBT man, this time he came out as a Trump supporter. He did it with style, rocking a MAGA-themed jacket at the 2019 Grammys, following in my footsteps as I cheered him on as a proud big sister.

We know we have a unique opportunity in Hollywood as musical artists and we're not afraid to be a little rough around the edges. After all, we're nobody's preachers, as he says. We're rock stars!

Anyway, Ricky is absolute pop royalty. He and I produced the song together. I took the lyrical helm and he took the musical helm, and I've felt absolutely fulfilled in creating it.

I urge and implore all my fans, followers, and readers: Use your voice over the chaos.

Use *your* voice—your beautiful, unique, individual voice—to pray and sing and celebrate goodness over the craziness.

Use your voice over destruction.

Use your voice over violence.

I stand against hatred in all its forms. Hate is a virus.

I stand against violence. It's not a solution.

But I stand *for* the American flag. Oh, yes.

I love this country and all of the opportunities it gives us every single day. We don't say that enough. But it's true.

God created each of us as equals—and equal under the American flag will we stay.

As proud Americans, and as conservatives who believe in this country's traditions and who want to preserve this nation for our future children and grandchildren, we need to use our voices for freedom and for a brighter future in this country.

We need voices over violence.

How I Began My Journey

Let me tell you more about the evening of February 8, 2017—and what happened to me after I dramatically came out for Trump and began my journey in kickass conservatism. After all, I'd been a liberal feminist for years (for too long!), so it was no small matter.

Because of my actions and statements on the red carpet that night, my album, "I Make The Static"—as I referenced earlier—skyrocketed to No. 1 in Alt, No. 1 in Rock, No. 7 in digital albums, and No. 12 in the Hot 200 on the Billboard Music Charts.

Hitting major milestones like these was a dream of mine since I started pursuing music professionally in 2011. It was a blessing—and to say I was over the moon about it is an understatement.

I also dominated the iTunes and Amazon music charts in only four days (the charts count seven days of sales). During that time, I outsold Beyoncé, Adele, and Lady Gaga.

I was positively freaking out with excitement and awe as texts, emails, and messages of support poured in from both devoted friends and complete strangers.

All of this, with *no label* or the millions and millions in advertisements that so many other artists have. I had known I'd cause a stir, but I'd never imagined my passionate and outspoken belief in our then-newly elected

Republican President, Donald J. Trump—the man who stunned the world and defeated liberal Democrat Hillary Rodham Clinton on November 8, 2016—would turn heads and make people sit up and take notice.

I think I snapped more necks than a car crash on the freeway!

With both my actions and my words, I surprised everyone. I was standing up for Trump—and suddenly people were paying attention.

Why? The answer, in part, is because I don't look anything like a traditional conservative.

Surprise!

'Kill Her!'

But it wasn't all sunshine and rainbows. After my red-carpet appearance and all the excitement it generated, my heart fell to my stomach as I received ghastly death threat after death threat. There were vows of violence, of the desire to do horrible things to me, to my body, to my family, to my home—all because of my support for this president.

There were cries of "Cancel her!"

People screamed, "Shave off that Afro!"

They yelled, "Kill her!"

These cries became regular from that day forward.

They continue today.

Yeah, baby, I get so many haters it would make your head spin.

Some days this awfulness threatens to overwhelm me and makes me feel small and dejected. I am a human being, after all, and I feel things deeply. (You'll see more about the haters and how to handle them later in this book.)

But then I remember that my purpose in this life is to shine brightly in this world, to be so brilliant and amazing that I help others in their own journey, help them communicate clearly with both themselves and with others—and thereby help change the political landscape in our country for the better.

And I am fighting every day to convey to people: Let me be who I am. Respect me for *me*. Don't try to shut me up. And don't try to limit my speech simply because you don't like it or disagree with it, as I've said in many media interviews.

Through my nearly four years now of being an out-and-proud conservative celebrity in Hollywood as an Afro-Latina woman, I've successfully learned how to deal with the horrible haters. I'll help you deal with them, too.

I've also done numerous interviews with Fox News, *People, The Hollywood Reporter, Variety, The Epoch Times*, and other outlets. Search results for my name post-Grammys in 2017 generated over 150 million hits in 24 hours!

And I didn't stop with one dress.

I just kept going.

(That's a quality I have, as you'll keep discovering within these pages. Oh, yeah!)

They Went Wild

I continued to shock the world and kept outdoing myself by coming out as pro-life. I announced on Twitter that abortion is murder. Then I shared my very own personal adoption story as a birth mom (more on that within these pages) with both Fox News and *People*.

I've talked about this and written about it a lot.

Then, at the next red carpet of the Grammy Awards—in 2018, in New York City—I wore a dress with my own handpainted image of my very own daughter in the womb, surrounded by beautifully colored lights.

And on my purse, I handpainted the words, "Choose Life."

The Daily Caller, in a headline about me, said my gown in 2018 "might be the most pro-life dress the red carpet has ever seen."

But the mainstream press and all the haters went *wild!*

I went on to wear a "Build the Wall" gown on the red carpet of the 2019 Grammy Awards.

I also wore two other pro-life statement dresses around this time: a fresh, green look supporting Save The Storks, one of my favorite pro-life charities, at the Daytime Emmy Awards in May 2019; and a tight, bubblegum-pink latex Barbie look at the film premiere of *Unplanned* just two months prior to that, in March 2019, when I boldly and unabashedly declared, "F*** Planned Parenthood." (Yes, I share a lot more about my pro-life stance later in this book!)

I've never shied away from boldness, to be clear.

The gowns I've just mentioned were all designed by my longtime designer, Desi Allinger of Desi Designs Couture.

Oh, and Planned Parenthood is responsible for over 80 percent of the brutal killings of unborn children in the U.S., to explain more about why I did what I did. The clinics often pressure young girls to abort their tiny babies even when the young women are in doubt about doing that. The organization aggressively targets Black neighborhoods. This is a genocidal travesty that breaks my heart and angers my soul every single day. And now Planned Parenthood has endorsed Democrat Joe Biden for president in November 2020. *This makes me sick.*

I had a falling out with my original dress designer in 2017, by the way. He couldn't take the haters—so he folded and turned against me.

It was heartbreaking, knowing that someone I'd trusted, worked with, and loved would cave so easily instead of defending me, especially when we created magic together. He and his family refused to see me or speak to me, even after I befriended First Daughter Ivanka Trump and was planning on introducing them so that she could possibly wear one of his beautiful creations. I still have so much love in my heart for him. And I understand. The business of being outspoken for freedom is not for everyone. It's a tough, hateful world filled with sharks.

But he's not the only dear friend I lost after I came out as conservative. A singer and songwriter from one of the former top pop groups of all time, someone I'd been friends with since 2015, confided in me that she was pro-Trump. I encouraged her to come out publicly, which she did. And then, after benefitting from my influence and news connections, she threw me under the bus once the haters came calling.

My mother called these types of people "fair-weather friends."

Many others turned their backs on me, even some family, once I came out as conservative and did so strongly and unapologetically.

I've been slandered.

Called a "coon."

A "race traitor."

A "betrayer."

I have even been called the N word—"a house n*****"—by my own people.

Meaning, *by my old people*. The liberals.

They *used to be* my people. They were the ones I thought were fighting for freedom—for human rights, women's rights, equality, free speech. Remember those days? Wasn't that long ago. (I'm a millennial, so I remember.)

But now, in this country, there's *only one party* that is truly fighting for freedom. Fighting for *your* freedom. *My* freedom.

That's the Republican Party.

And since President Trump is a Republican, then I'm a Trumplican! Millions upon millions of other Americans are, too.

Read it and weep, liberal Dems.

To all those liberals who say they hate our country, hate Trump, hate conservatives, I say: *Move out of the country, please.*

I know I'm going to piss off a lot of my Hollywood friends and peers, but if you hate it so much, *you can leave.*

And if they think socialism really works—well, then they can go find it in other countries and see how well it's worked there.

None of this negativity from others ultimately deters me, by the way.

I hope it doesn't deter you, either. We can be taken aback momentarily by some of it, even seriously shocked by a lot of it. But these attitudes are something we must acknowledge and deal with head-on.

I stand by my beliefs and my full support of President Trump. I believe 100 percent in the American dream and how important our values and integrity are to this nation. I believe 100 percent in a strong America. And I've made a successful career of speaking and creating music, films, and messages that inspire and educate others on these and other conservative-driven topics.

You might have already known that bit of my personal history.

But of course, there's more.

And there is much more to *your* story as a conservative, too—especially in 2020.

Getting Paid to Wreak Havoc?

As our nation continues to debate and discuss police reform in the wake of George Floyd's death, liberals and progressives are up in arms against law enforcement in this country—the overwhelming majority of whom are good, hardworking, and upstanding people trying to do an almost impossible job as best they can.

And now there's a whole contingent of progressives who are defacing and tearing down monuments and other important commemorations of

American history across our country. As I told Jesse Watters of Fox News about this issue right after the violence three years ago in Charlottesville, Virginia, we should *not* get rid of our statues. Just because we have a statue of someone or something doesn't mean we're always celebrating what happened. Instead, some of these physical monuments are remembrances of pivotal moments in our history—just as with 9/11 memorials.

Trying to erase history is not putting us forward. It's actually putting us backward. Besides, attacking and destroying statues is *unlawful*.

President Trump, in fact, just signed a new executive order to protect American monuments, memorials, and statues across the country. And on the eve of July 4 this year, at a spectacular, pro-America event at Mount Rushmore in South Dakota—an event that the leftists naturally criticized—the president said that "those who seek to erase our heritage want Americans to forget our pride and our great dignity, so that we can no longer understand ourselves or America's destiny."

Yes—he called them out!

Trump also announced that he wants to create a new national park to display statues and monuments dedicated to "American Heroes."

Instead of tearing down things in America, we need to *build up* America, as I also told Jesse Watters. Let's stop destroying things that offend us, admit the parts of our history that are bad, and celebrate the people who fought to make our country a better place for all of us.

I feel that it's important we recognize the role played by members of the domestic terror group Antifa and all of the radical, far-left liberals who have thrown in with these destructive anarchists.

It's my belief that people have been getting paid—*are* getting paid—to take part in destructive riots and other violent actions in this country.

I know we'll continue to hear more about this issue for the rest of this year and beyond. The lockdowns and curfews imposed on American citizens this year because of the coronavirus scourge that came here from China have only added to a sense of fear, helplessness, and chaos that many people are feeling.

But Donald Trump is a law-and-order president. He campaigned on that, and he's fighting for our country and for every one of us. He is standing up for the U.S.A. every day. The liberal media give him *so little credit* for all that he does.

Actually, they give him *no* credit at all.

They attack him, period.

Trump announced on May 31 of this year that the U.S. government seeks to designate Antifa as a terrorist organization. That designation would allow federal law enforcement agencies to target the entire sick group that is sowing so much discord among so many well-intentioned protesters.

Yet even as he and Attorney General William Barr discuss the government's efforts to go after "violent radical agitators," our president's voice is being silenced and suppressed on social media because liberals don't like him or his views. And it's not just that they don't like him, or that they disagree with his views, his political stances. They *hate* him.

All of these realities and more, at this volatile time in America, are why we need everyone to stand up for what they truly believe.

We need to help our country and, in the process, help ourselves.

One Nation Under God

We need you in this movement. We need more people who believe in our country and aren't afraid to say that.

Remember, today's modern conservatives can look like anything. We can be anybody.

We defy stereotyping.

We are Americans, first of all—and we believe in America, even with its flaws and the hard times we've been going through all this year and before.

There have been hard times in the past and there will be more in the future. We must stay strong no matter what. We are working toward a better tomorrow.

Our country, despite our hardships, is the greatest country on the face of the earth. We need to remind ourselves of its goodness and fight for its preservation. This is why conservatism is so important—and why I joined its ranks four years ago. This is why I'm a kickass conservative!

Today's modern conservatives are young. They're gay. They're Black. They're Latin American. They're of so many varying backgrounds I can't even name them all here.

And that's the point: We're *Americans*. We're all part of this big, beautiful country.

We can have tattoos.

We can have piercings.

We can be anyone.

Kickass conservatives can look like me!

Everyone is welcome as a conservative. Above all, we conservatives care about traditional values. We love our country and we want it to flourish for years and years to come, for ourselves and for all those we love.

Today's conservatives are assertive. We're aggressive. We represent one nation.

We have the rights of freedom of speech, freedom of religion, and so many other freedoms as outlined in the Bill of Rights—and we like it that way and want to keep it that way.

If you believe in all of these things and more, then you're *in*.

And if you believe in Trump and believe he is the person who is going to continue to make this country greater than it's ever been—and that our best days are ahead of us—you're in.

There's no "requirement" to be White, Christian, male, or of a certain age to be a conservative.

Those days are long gone—long over.

Sure, there are still plenty of buttoned-up, pencil-pocket, pearl-wearing conservatives in America. That's totally fine! People are free to be who they are, and I'll put my arm around any conservative any time.

But what is true is that we need everybody's passion, voices, and efforts to help preserve America at a time when it's facing so many challenges.

And we must reelect Trump this fall.

Let me tell you how you can stand up for conservative values and all that's great about America—and be your truest self—at a most crucial time in our history. Along the way, you can be the sassiest, sexiest, most kickass conservative ever!

NOW, HERE'S MY REAL-LIFE TIP FOR YOU (the first of many in this book) for leading a great life: Don't you want to accomplish your dreams? Feel supported in your efforts? Achieve unbelievable success? Find amazing happiness and unlimited good health?

Of course you do! We all do. No one starts out in life thinking they want to be mediocre. That would be ridiculous.

So let's acknowledge and respect that we *all* want to achieve greatness in our own ways, as we see it. And that no one should stop us from doing that.

By the same token, don't you want a great country? A place where all of our citizens—no matter their beliefs, their backgrounds, their looks, their loves—are respected, honored, and given every opportunity?

A nation where we feel united? A place that offers all of us a grand slate of amazing possibilities? A place that we're proud to call home?

Of course you do! We all do.

Join me on this path of committed conservatism in America.

Stand up to those who would try to silence us.

Be a kickass conservative—and proud of it.

This book outlines just how I did it—and how you can, too.

And here's more inspiration.

Here are the lyrics of my new song with Ricky Rebel. Please read every word of my song! (Find it on all music platforms and on www.joyvilla.com.)

"VOICE OVER VIOLENCE"
by Joy Villa, featuring Ricky Rebel

Don't gotta be perfect
Don't gotta be perfect
Rise like the burning sun

Won't know that it's worth it
Won't know that it's worth it
Until the fight is won

Shattered dreams
Brick by brick
No one wins
When we're sick

(We need a)
Voice over violence

Singing out in the crowd
Won't you join us now

Voice over violence

Voice over violence
Coming out of the dark
Open up your heart

Hate is a virus
Voice over violence

Time to take real action
Get a new reaction
Speak or move out the way

All various colors
My sisters and brothers
Listen to what I say

Shattered dreams
Brick by brick
No one wins
When we're sick

(We need a)
Voice over violence
Singing out in the crowd
Won't you join us now

Voice over violence

Voice over violence
Coming out of the dark
Open up your heart

Hate is a virus
Voice over violence

We need to
Break through the silence
Standing side by side

We need a
Voice over violence
We can
End the divide

(We need a)
Voice over violence
Singing out in the crowd
Won't you join us now

Voice over violence

Voice over violence
Coming out of the dark
Open up your heart

Hate is a virus
Voice over violence

We need your voice
We have no choice

Voice over violence

. . . .

CHAPTER 2

How I Met the President and Why I'm a Passionate Trumplican

Hint: I Love America and I Hate B.S.

"I was elected to represent the citizens of Pittsburgh, not Paris."
—President Donald J. Trump

P EOPLE OFTEN ASK ME, "Why do you keep speaking out for Trump?"
Did they ever say that to supporters of Barack Obama, by the way?
Did they ever constantly, repeatedly, *endlessly* question liberals for backing Obama for two terms and eight years?

Please.

I'm going to answer that, and I'll share a few personal stories that will shed light on this, too.

Meeting President Trump was a most incredible thing for me, and it was the opportunity and privilege of a lifetime.

The first time I met the president was at a White House Christmas Party on December 11, 2017.

He came out and greeted me. He greeted everybody there.

He was so kind.

Bet this is something you've never heard about our president. The liberal media won't say it, that's for sure.

Trump is a kind man. It is immediately obvious in person.

He spoke a few words to all of us about what Christmas means to him. He talked about his Christian faith and his family.

And it was a beautiful time.

The president is statuesque and strong, with a hearty handshake and an easy smile. And First Lady Melania Trump is graceful and beautiful. She made a short appearance and then went back.

You could tell that the First Couple were in their element. It was their first Christmas at the White House, and the party was a sparkling, effervescent affair.

First Daughter Ivanka Trump was also at the party, and I was happy to take some pictures with her. She's incredible—tall and classy. She was wearing a beautiful burgundy dress that evening. I met some of her family and friends that she grew up with; she introduced me to them.

I was there with my now-ex-husband, Thorsten, who is a great photographer and took photos of the event.

It truly felt like a dream. And I felt like the belle of the ball.

Many of Trump's biggest supporters and donors were there, and they came up with hugs and handshakes. We laughed together and shared some fantastic moments.

The lovely evening is forever etched in my mind.

I'll cherish it always.

The second time I met the president was at the Faith and Freedom Coalition "Road to Majority" policy event in Washington, D.C., on June 26, 2019. The president pointed me out and said hello to me from the stage.

Here I am with First Daughter Ivanka Trump, an amazing woman, at the White House Christmas Party in 2017.

And I got to see him again at that event.

Then the third time I saw the president was right after that. It was back at the White House for its Social Media Summit on July 11, 2019—which was historic for a number of reasons.

That's the day, out in the Rose Garden and in front of the cameras, that I wound up telling off some obnoxious members of the press who were, and still are, engaged in publishing fake news and who didn't like having to bump elbows with truth-telling social media personalities like myself!

The president, ever gracious, said to all of us at the event, "Together, you reach more people than any television broadcast, BY FAR!"

That's something the president himself tweeted about the summit.

And at the summit inside the White House, the president also said, "Hey, Joy, I just saw you."

He said it from the podium.

He pointed me out and said, "Stand up. You always look amazing in those dresses."

"There she is, my Hollywood star," he added. "She's always shining and she looks great. And she's got this dress with—in big letters—it says 'Trump' on it."

Then he said, "*She's* not big—she's tiny. It's the letters that are big!"

Everyone laughed.

And all of this was extra funny because I'm 5'10." I'm his daughter's height, with strong, muscular legs.

It felt so feminine and comforting to me to be called "tiny" by President Trump, since I'm so tall!

I tweeted that day about what the president said to me.

It felt like he was my father in that moment.

And I do believe he is America's daddy, and I don't care how contro-

realdonaldtrump
The White House

6/10

♡ ○ ▽   ⊔

Liked by **stephenfleming91** and **84,727 others**

realdonaldtrump Each of you is fulfilling a vital role in our nation – you are challenging the media gatekeepers and the corporate censors to bring the facts straight to the American People. Together, you reach more people than any television broadcast, BY FAR! #SocialMediaSummit

versial it sounds to say that. It's the truth. He is that strong father figure that everybody needs in their life. And that's why many leftists rebel against him, because he's insisting on ethics for those who need it the most.

We've needed a strong father to run America for so long. This country has been left with weak men—and, as a result, struggling and tired women and messed-up children.

Anyway, the president continued to brag on me in front of others as I blushed. He said, "She does it with a smile, even though she gets all that hate. She just keeps on going."

He added, "Joy Villa. She's amazing, everybody."

He continued to compliment me for what seemed like an eternity.

I'm being honest here with you, as I always am and will be throughout this book. It was the most incredible feeling to be at the White House and wearing my red, white, and blue freedom dress, which was specially made for me by my designer, Desi Allinger. There were perhaps only 100 other guests there. And there I was, praised publicly as a social media superstar by the president. So, yes, I will say it here: It was a really big deal!

Later, when President Trump and I were standing near each other, he said to me, "Yeah, Hollywood," and I smiled and thanked him.

I said to him, "You know, you have more support in Hollywood than you know, Mr. President. You have a lot of support there."

And he said, "I know. It's because they like my tax breaks."

The people around us erupted in laughter.

The president was warm, he was jovial, he was friendly, and he was, above all, kind. He made me feel like the most important person in that room.

He celebrated me, he complimented me, and he validated me.

He recognized me for who I am and for what I've done.

I've been working hard for a man who's worked harder than anyone else for us and in this country. So, yes, it's my absolute pleasure to help and serve a leader like this.

It is my honor to know the president of the United States. And I do feel that it's a duty to be able to serve this country.

Warrior Spirit

That's why I lift up our military every chance I get for that sense of pride, honor, and service to our country and to our commander-in-chief that they embrace.

It's what my own father, as a Vietnam-era Army veteran, instilled in me from an early age.

I will never forget my father's love of this country. And the fortitude and strength to continue loving this country now comes from President Trump. The president of the United States—my president and my friend, Donald J. Trump—conveyed this to me during those moments in the White House.

He's not just my president. *He is my friend.* And he admires me as much as I admire him, which is an incredible thing.

There is an air of dignity about our president, but no air of arrogance. He was jovial that day, full of humor and confidence.

Here's a man who exudes so much B.D.E. (Yeah, I'm saying this!) Trump exudes that warrior spirit, that energy and masculinity.

He also has the spiritual strength to lead our nation, even though our

At the White House Social Media Summit, with Jesse Holguin, founder of LEXIT, and Diamond and Silk.

great nation is too often filled with, at best, brats who despise him and, at worst, rats who try to undermine him.

Trump also stands for all the forgotten people, the people in the fly-over states, the ones Hillary Clinton so rudely and wrongly called "deplorables" (something we'll never forget, by the way). That's people like me, writing this book—and maybe people like you, reading this book.

We're the folks who were and *are* forgotten and unspoken for, the ones Hollywood calls "disgusting," the ones who are ignored by so many liberal snobs and Democrat elites.

We're the hard workers of this country.

We're the hardworking people no matter where we're located, in the farmlands, outside the cities, you name it. We're the stay-at-home, home-schooling moms; the stay-at-home, strong-provider dads; the devoted families; the dedicated churchgoers; the absolute followers of goodness; the enthusiastic flag wavers; the believers and defenders of the Second Amendment; and the true, salt-of-the-earth Americans who made our country great.

We're the ones who are looked down upon by the liberals, by the Democrats, by the mainstream media, and by those in Hollywood—yet we're taxed like crazy and written off as unimportant and inconsequential.

We're the people the president never forgot. We're the people he fought for in 2016 and the ones he's fighting for again in 2020. We're the ones he campaigned for and the people who voted him into the White House—and the ones who will vote to *keep* him in the White House for another four years.

This is why I love this president so much. He knows America. He cherishes our country. He's fighting for our country. He wants it to be as strong as it can possibly be.

And it's why I will follow this man into his second term as he leads this nation to victory for Americans of all colors, all shapes, all sizes, all ethnicities, and all sexualities.

The president does not discriminate.

This is a president who blends old-school conservative beliefs with many socially moderate ideas—and he has the wild audacity to confront Hillary Clinton and her swampy crime network. He has the audacity to kick disgraced director Harvey Weinstein out of Mar-a-Lago, and he nominates a conservative Supreme Court justice—Brett Kavanaugh—who is a strong, masculine, parental figure.

Trump does not kowtow to the #cancelledmoms of the world.

Above all, he is boldly, unapologetically **AMERICAN**.

Growing Strong and Staying Strong

The president has tweeted me a number of times—eight or nine times, I think. Each time it's been incredible and has meant so much to me.

This is a man who makes me proud that I voted for him, even though I'll admit that I—as someone who thought she was a liberal for years—did have a few doubts early on, back in the early fall of 2016 and before that.

There was so much I didn't know then.

Whatever doubts I had then quickly disappeared once I realized that Trump didn't just talk the talk.

During those early days, I know I was playing it very #safe. Remember, I'd spent so much time in the liberal world—so when I came out publicly in support of Trump, I did so almost apologetically for a while. And in a tweet back then, showing just how safe I was trying to play it, I even called him one of "the crazy candidates" who was out there.

That's how things went. I'm being honest with all of you on this, as I always am.

I know who I was then, and I know who I am *now*. I was trying to be diplomatic in those days. I was scared to death of the leftist mob—I'll say it again. I had worked so hard to build my music career as an independent and strong woman in Hollywood, and I feared they would "cancel" me.

Sad, right, what these people do to others or threaten to do?

And it wasn't until April 2017—two months after I came out strongly for Trump at the Grammys that year—that I took the word "feminist" off my Twitter bio and my other social media bios. It took months for me to be really strong and confident about sharing my conservative beliefs publicly.

It took time for me to learn and to grow in that way.

This is not an overnight change—it wasn't an overnight change for me from liberalism back to conservatism (I had started off as a conservative when I was very young).

I'm making all of this clear because sometimes people don't understand that coming out as a conservative can be a process.

It may be a process for you as well.

I am not a conservative in word only; my actions speak louder than any word or label possibly could. I am not a Republican in name only; I detest people who are in this merely for the fame or glory of it.

And if, in fact, I went to CNN or MSNBC at this very moment and said something like, "Hey, I'm no longer a Trump supporter. What do you think?"—and to be clear, *this is something I would never do*—well, I'd be on every magazine cover, every website, and every social media feed almost instantly. Those liberals would lap it up and lord it over everyone forever.

In 2017, I was handpicked by Lara Trump to be on the president's Campaign Advisory Board. It was a tremendous honor for me. I proudly served on that board, working alongside Lara and the team, and helped to further the president's messages to the American people. (Once I started an exploratory committee, when I was looking at possibly running for Congress in 2018, I had to bring my time on that team to a close.)

Today, I'm proud to be a member of a number of groups, including Black Voices for Trump and the White House National Hispanic Community. I've made more than 40 appearances on major media outlets, including Fox News, to speak out about Trump and conservative values. My zeal for the conservative movement has not wavered after four years.

I'm friendly with Ivanka Trump and Lara Trump and I'm proud to know them and see them regularly. I've also met Don Jr. and Eric Trump. They are all strong, loyal, red-blooded Americans who—along with our great president—want to make our country better.

Our country needs to reelect President Trump this fall and to have him lead us again for four more years—and to help bring along other conservative political leaders who will take us far beyond that.

A Trump Speech to Remember

There may be no better illustration of how well Trump represents America, how he defends the freedoms we enjoy in our country, and why I fervently support this president than the speech Trump gave on Memorial Day of this year—May 25, 2020—at Fort McHenry in Baltimore, Maryland.

Trump's Memorial Day appearance and speech are now terribly overshadowed by the death of George Floyd later that very same day (Floyd died around 9:30 p.m. on the night of May 25, 2020).

I've already explained my thoughts about Floyd's death.

And as I've said, I believe in Black lives. I believe in police lives.

But what I want to say here about Memorial Day—so that it is *not lost* among so much else—is that Fort McHenry was the site that served as inspiration for Francis Scott Key more than 200 years ago, when Key wrote "The Star-Spangled Banner," which later, of course, became our national anthem.

(Shortly before I finalized my book, anarchists in San Francisco's Golden Gate Park tore down a statue of Francis Scott Key after covering it in anti-slavery and anti-colonizer graffiti. Destruction and criminal activity like this are abhorrent to me.)

Our great country deserves our support, our protection, and our love. This is what Trump acts on every day, and I thank God for him.

With Lara Trump, a great American. I'm very proud to know this lady!

I loved Trump's Memorial Day speech. It gave me chills.

As I watched it, it made me choke up. I loved how he stood up for us—and for our country. I loved how American flags flew right behind him in a spectacular backdrop as he delivered his remarks.

On such a solemn occasion, I appreciated how our president, as well as our wonderful First Lady Melania Trump, paid their respects to America's fallen heroes—and to all those in the military and across our country who have been risking their own lives to save others. That includes how they've been risking their lives during the coronavirus pandemic. All of us can adapt. We *will* adapt. We *are* adapting.

And let me tell you further why my heart swells with patriotism and love of our country. Want to know how this president stands up for each of us every day of the year? Then read his Memorial Day speech *in its entirety.*

Even if you saw it live on TV when he delivered it, read it here in my book. In this book, the speech is forever. The liberal mainstream media barely covered the speech. *Sad*—and bad on them! The speech is vintage Trump and it's vintage America.

Read it to remind yourself of some of our outstanding history. Read it to learn, here and now, how this president, more than many of his predecessors, believes in our freedoms, our future as Americans, and in making and keeping this country as strong and as great as our Founders knew it could be, would be, and still can be. *Forever.*

Remember, the liberals and progressives don't want you to know the good stuff about the president! And many of these people—not all, but many—are trying to destroy our country as we know it.

And if you and I speak up and push back, they won't succeed.

With this book, you have Trump's Memorial Day speech forever in one place, so you can read it now and come back to it whenever you want.

Take solace from it—use it to inspire your own actions and behavior.

President Trump's Memorial Day Speech

Delivered on May 25, 2020, at Fort McHenry National Monument and Historic Shrine, in Baltimore, Maryland

(THE PRESIDENT): I stand before you at this noble fortress of American liberty to pay tribute to the immortal souls who fought and died to keep us free.

Earlier today, the First Lady and I laid a wreath in their sacred honor at Arlington National Cemetery. Now we come together to salute the flag they gave their lives to so boldly and brilliantly defend.

And we pledge in their cherished memories that this majestic flag will proudly fly forever.

We're joined for today's ceremony by Secretary of Defense Mark Esper, Secretary of the Interior David Bernhardt, the Chairman of the Joint Chiefs of Staff General Mark Milley, Congressman Andy Harris, and a number of servicemembers and veterans of the Armed Forces.

The dignity, daring, and devotion of the American military is unrivaled anywhere in history and any place in the world.

In recent months, our nation and the world have been engaged in a new form of battle against an invisible enemy. Once more, the men and women of the United States military have answered the call to duty and raced into danger. Tens of thousands of servicemembers and National Guardsmen are on the front lines of our war against this terrible virus, caring for patients, delivering critical supplies, and working night and day to safeguard our citizens.

As one nation, we mourn alongside every single family that has lost loved ones, including the families of our great veterans. Together, we will vanquish the virus, and America will rise from this crisis to new and even greater heights.

As our brave warriors have shown us from the nation's earliest days, in America, we are the captains of our own fate. No obstacle, no challenge, and no threat is a match for the sheer determination of the American people. This towering spirit permeates every inch of the hollowed soil beneath our feet.

In this place more than 200 years ago, American patriots stood their ground and repelled a British invasion in the Battle of Baltimore, during the War of 1812. Early on a September morning in 1814, the British fleet launched an assault on this peninsula. From the harbor, some 30 British warships attacked this stronghold. Rockets rained down. Bombs burst in the air. In the deck of one ship, a gallant young American was held captive. His name was Francis Scott Key.

For 25 hours, Key watched in dismay as fire crashed down upon this ground. But through torrents of rain and smoke and the din of battle, Key could make out 15 broad stripes and 15 bright stars barraged and battered—but still there.

American forces did not waver. They did not retreat. They stared down the invasion and they held. They had to endure. The fact is they held like nobody could have held before. They held this fort. The British retreated. Independence was saved.

Francis Scott Key was so inspired by the sight of our flag in the battle waged that the very grounds that he fought on became hallowed. And he wrote a poem. His ageless words became the anthem of our nation, "The Star-Spangled Banner."

Every time we sing our anthem, every time its rousing chorus swells our hearts with pride, we renew the eternal bonds of loyalty to our fallen heroes. We think of the soldiers who spend their final heroic moments on distant battlefields to keep us safe at home. We remember the young Americans who never got the chance to grow old but whose legacy will outlive us all.

In every generation, these intrepid souls kissed goodbye to their families and loved ones. They took flight in planes, set sail in ships, and marched into battle with our flag, fighting for our country, defending our people.

When the cause of liberty was in jeopardy, American warriors carried that flag through ice and snow to victory at Trenton. They hoisted it up the mass of great battleships in Manila Bay. They fought through hell to raise it high atop a remote island in the Pacific Ocean called Iwo Jima. From the Philippine Sea to Fallujah, from New Orleans to Normandy, from Saratoga to Saipan, from the Battle of Baltimore to the Battle of the Bulge, Americans gave their lives to carry that flag through piercing waves, blazing fires, sweltering deserts, and storms of bullets and shrapnel. They climbed atop enemy tanks, jumped out of burning airplanes, and leaped on live grenades. Their love was boundless. Their devotion was without limit. Their courage was beyond measure.

Army Green Beret Captain Daniel Eggers grew up in Cape Coral, Florida, determined to continue his family tradition of military service. And it was a great tradition. He attended the legendary Citadel Military College in South Carolina. Soon, he met a beautiful cadet, Rebecca. They fell in love, married, and had two sons.

In 2004, Daniel left for his second deployment in Afghanistan. On the morning of May 29th, Daniel and his team were courageously pursuing a group of deadly terrorists when he was killed by an improvised explosive device. This week is the 16th anniversary of the day that Daniel made the supreme sacrifice for our nation. He laid down his life to defeat evil and to save his fellow citizens.

At the time of his death, Daniel's sons, Billy and John, were three and five years old. Today, they have followed in Daniel's footsteps—both students at the Citadel, planning to serve in the military. They're amazing. Mom Rebecca has now served more than 23 years in the U.S. Army. Everywhere she goes, she wears Daniel's Gold Star pin on the lapel of her uniform.

Colonel Rebecca Eggers and her two sons are here today, along with Daniel's father, Bill, and mother Margot. To the entire Eggers family, your sacrifice is beyond our ability to comprehend or repay. Today, we honor Daniel's incredible life and exceptional valor, and we promise you that we will treasure his blessed memory forever. Thank you very much for being here. Thank you very much. (Applause.)

Please. Thank you. Thank you.

Great family. Thank you very much.

To every Gold Star family here today and all across our land, our debt to you is infinite and everlasting. We stand with you today and all days to come remembering and grieving for America's greatest heroes. In spirit and strength, in loyalty and love, in character and courage, they were larger than life itself. They were angels sent from above, and they are now rejoined with God in the glorious Kingdom of Heaven.

Wherever the Stars and Stripes fly at our schools, our

churches, town halls, firehouses, and national monuments, it is made possible because there are extraordinary Americans who are willing to brave death so that we can live in freedom and live in peace.

In the two centuries since Francis Scott Key wrote about the stirring sight of our flag in battle, countless other American patriots have given their own testimony about the meaning of the flag.

One was World War II veteran Jim Krebs, from Sunbury, Ohio. Jim and his twin brother, Jack, fought side by side in General Patton's Third Army at the Battle of the Bulge. The twins volunteered for a dangerous mission. Together they took out four enemy tanks, two machine gun nests, and a mothar [sic] position that was very powerful, loaded up with mortars. Jim's brother Jack was mortally wounded Jim held his dying brother in his arms, praying together as his twin passed away.

Jim fought to victory and came home to build a great American life. He married, had children, became an electrical engineer, and taught young people about war. As an old man, Jim was asked about the American flag and what it meant to him. Jim said, "The flag to me is as precious as the freedom that the flag stands for. It's as precious to me as the thousands of lives that have been lost defending her. It's that important to me; it gave me a value of life that I could have never gotten any other way. It gave me a value of my Lord, my family, my friends, loved ones, and especially my country. What more could I ask?"

Last month, Jim died peacefully at his home at the age

of 94. This afternoon we are greatly honored to be joined by his grandsons, Andy and Ron. Please, thank you very much. Thank you very much. (Applause.) Thank you very much for being here.

Today, as we remember the sacrifices of Jim's brother Jack, we honor Jim's service, and we are moved by his beautiful words. Andy and Ron, thank you for being here to remember your grandfather and his brother, and what they did for us all, and most importantly what they stood for.

From generation to generation, heroes like these have poured out their blood and sweat and heart and tears for our country. Because of them, America is strong and safe and mighty and free. Because of them, two centuries on, the Star-Spangled Banner still proudly waves.

For as long as our flag flies in the sky above, the names of these fallen warriors will be woven into its threads. For as long as we have citizens willing to follow their example, to carry on their burden, to continue their legacy, then America's cause will never fail and American freedom will never, ever die.

Today, we honor the heroes we have lost. We pray for the loved ones they left behind. And with God as our witness, we solemnly vow to protect, preserve, and cherish this land they gave their last breath to defend and to defend so proudly.

Thank you. God bless our military. God bless the memory of the fallen. God bless our Gold Star families. And God bless America.

Thank you very much. (Applause.)

(END OF SPEECH)

Isn't that one of the most *beautiful* speeches you've ever read or heard?

These remarks by the president—and so many more of his words, his actions, and his beliefs ever since his election as our commander-in-chief—are why I support him.

And this is why I'm giving a voice to the voiceless in my support of him.

I want to help all of you know that *you have permission to support him and the conservative movement.*

That's something—again—that the liberals will never tell you. But *I'm* telling you.

On Memorial Day, Trump was talking about the soldiers who have given their lives for this country. And guess what? These fallen soldiers would be appalled to know what's going on this year—and that our country has been shut down for so long over a Chinese virus that *China mishandled and threw in our faces.*

And now China has been telling us all that we should fix the problem by dumping boatloads of cash into the WHO.

Trump announced a freeze on funding for the group and he's accused the WHO of bias toward China.

And now, he's begun the process of officially withdrawing the U.S. from the WHO, to take effect in July 2021. Keep an eye on all of this.

I'm not a conspiracy theorist, even though people will say I am. But we must follow Trump's lead. We must be pro-America. And we must question the spending of billions of dollars for the agendas of other people and other entities.

Fight for Free Speech!

At every turn, we must also fight for free speech. I say this in part because of what's been happening on social media this year.

Facebook has said it's going to start labeling certain posts as malicious news and malicious misinformation. If you say in a post on Facebook, "I used zinc and hydroxychloroquine to combat the coronavirus"—which the president has taken this year, by the way, and I trust this president; I don't trust anyone else in the government. I trust Trump—and if you say, "A doctor in Los Angeles has used this medical treatment, and it's helping his patients," well, that comment gets banned and Facebook will take it away because the platform "believes" that your comments are dangerous misinformation.

That is insane.

And it's especially insane because a new hydroxychloroquine study that's just out *has proved that the president was right about the drug.*

And look at what Twitter began doing in May to President Trump!

It "fact-checked" his tweets when he wrote about the fraud problems connected to mail-in voting, something the Democrats want so very badly.

Twitter has also slapped "warning" labels on other Trump tweets.

Yet Twitter's so-called "head of site integrity" *(what is that?)* is a virulent anti-Trumper. Right after Trump was elected in 2016, this individual wrote on Twitter, "I'm just saying, we fly over those states that voted for a racist tangerine for a reason."

Despicable.

This person also wrote, "Yes, that person in the pink hat is clearly a bigger threat to your brand of feminism than actual NAZIS IN THE WHITE HOUSE."

And these people are censoring the president?

We Trump supporters must continue to speak out.

We must have freedom of speech.

We must voice our opinions.

We must stand up for our country.

We cannot be shut down.

NOW, HERE'S MY REAL-LIFE TIP FOR YOU for being a Trumplican in 2020: Speak your true beliefs.

Share them with others.

Speak up for what you believe.

Speak up for this president.

Don't allow others to silence you.

I know this can be hard in many cases, depending on where you live, where you work, who you're connected to, and so much more. There's a lot of craziness out there right now.

I'm not going to minimize that. I understand that many people are afraid.

But do what you can in your own life, in your own circumstances, and in your own circles.

Use your God-given voice.

Most of all: *Vote for Trump in 2020.*

And beware the platforms and places where free speech is being compromised or shut down today. This is just common sense.

It's why I don't put all my eggs in one basket on social media. I have my own site and my own way of communicating with my fans, my followers, my friends, and so many others.

Consider how you, too, can reach others without being labeled, edited, or fact-checked by those with a political agenda.

· ·

CHAPTER 3

Death Threats and Haterade

The Secrets of Handling the Haters

"How much easier it is to be critical than to be correct."
—Benjamin Disraeli

P EOPLE OFTEN ASK ME, "As a conservative in Hollywood, isn't it awful for you to get all the hate that liberals throw your way? How do you deal with it?"

My answer to that is, I've got to speak out—and I'm going to keep doing it. We've got to say what we believe in America or we're going to lose our country.

I feel an obligation to speak forthrightly about my beliefs. America is and must remain the country of free speech. So I'm going to exercise my First Amendment rights every moment I'm here on this earth.

My second answer is, as an entertainer, an artist, a writer—and as an American, *period*—I don't allow myself to be muzzled.

As I mentioned earlier, I very publicly departed from the left, the liberals, and the Democrats in February 2017 when I unveiled my MAGA dress on the red carpet of the Grammys.

But that was just the beginning for me. I've done so much more since then, and my passion for speaking my mind continues to this day.

In the aftermath of showing off my MAGA dress in early 2017, I made other attention-getting fashion statements at various red-carpet events. In early 2018, I wore a dramatic pro-life dress to the Grammy Awards (more about this in my next chapter!). In 2019, I wore a dress about protecting America's borders that boldly declared, "Build the Wall!"

And this year, in February 2020 (which seems *soooo* long ago as I write this, though it was only months ago), I wore a "Trump 2020" dress. And was proud to do it.

I'm repeating some of this on purpose in this book, by the way. I carefully thought out and planned each of these steps, each of these moves, for a reason, and I want you all to know that.

And yep, I did what I did during those red-carpet appearances to get attention. That's what the red carpet is all about!

I've also done many television, print, and online interviews to share my viewpoints and beliefs. I've written op-eds and articles. I've talked to fans and followers on numerous live chats and social media events. I've tweeted and shared posts on Instagram and more.

Along the way, I've gotten evil eyes and "side eyes" from all kinds of people. And some of those people have been vulgar, using the F-word against me, calling me a "traitor" and much worse.

So, yes, the haters have made themselves known—and it's not a good look for them.

But I keep pushing.

I don't care what anyone thinks and none of us should.

I refuse to compromise my beliefs, my values, and my positions simply because a few profane loudmouths have a problem with what I say.

So keep reading, because I'm going to tell you exactly how to handle

At the Grammys in early 2020—so proud to stand up for our remarkable president!

those loudmouths. It's really important to have a plan and a process so that you don't get sucked in—or sucker-punched—by those of ill will.

Can't Keep Quiet

When I first came out as a Trump supporter, I was scared to do it because of all the bullying out there, as I noted. But I felt strongly about my positions, and by then I'd decided I could no longer keep quiet.

And shortly after that, when Brandon Straka and his #WalkAway campaign (www.walkawaycampaign.com) arrived fresh on the scene in 2018, I felt drawn to it and wanted to support it.

That was an extra shot of adrenaline for me. I am so grateful for it.

Like me, Brandon—an actor and someone I'm proud to call a friend—had embraced liberal values earlier in his life. But no longer believing in the left's empty promises, he chose to decisively and publicly #WalkAway from the Democrat Party and all of its echo-chamber proponents.

I attended many great #WalkAway events, spoke at those events, and addressed the cheering and supportive crowds that came to see us and hear our messages.

To this day, I tell my followers and all those interested in conservatism: It's OK to be different. Whatever you are and wherever you come from—if you're Black, Latino, gay, straight, Christian, Muslim, whatever you are—it's OK to walk away from the left.

It's OK to align yourself with those of us who care about the future of our country and want what's best for it—and for us.

It's not only OK to do this. It may be *your destiny.*

It's the most authentic feeling in the world when you live out your destiny!

And if you believe in Trump and support his pro-America, pro-freedom policies, come join us.

There is room for every single one of us in the conservative movement. But this is *not* true of the left today.

The left is no longer moderate. Anyone who is part of the left cannot think differently from that crowd. They must tow the line or they're out.

To me, it's a dictatorship. The liberal left wants people to think and say exactly as they do—and they don't tolerate much divergence, or *any* divergence, from their points of view.

I believe that those on the left are very much the fascists that they keep calling us. This and so much more is why I walked away from all that nonsense, embraced my true conservatism, voted for Trump in November 2016—and will vote for him again in November 2020.

'You've Changed Me'

Today's conservatives are more diverse, more inclusive, and more fashionable than those in years gone by.

I don't mean any disrespect to anyone by saying this. I'm simply pointing out that the movement today is resonating with a lot of young people of all backgrounds.

I've seen it. I've experienced it. I've witnessed their passion, their enthusiasm, and their commitment to conservative beliefs.

After some of the town halls I did in 2018 and 2019, people came up to me and said, "Wow, you've changed my viewpoint. You've changed *me*."

Plenty of young people in their 20s and 30s have told me that because of their skin color or their backgrounds, they thought they "had" to be liberal. They thought it was their only choice. A requirement. The only path for them.

They thought they *had* to espouse liberal viewpoints because there was no other way for them, no other lifestyle choice, no other political choice.

That is just not true.

As a person of mixed heritage and as someone who spent time in the liberal movement, I'm here to say: #WalkAway from that type of mindset. Believe what you want to believe.

And understand you have choices—some good ones. Great ones!

Be your God-given self. Support whomever you want to support, and live your life with all the independence you deserve. *This is 2020!*

I have been in their shoes—perhaps in your shoes—so I know how it feels. I know how it feels to be stuck. That is how I *used* to be and how my life *used* to be. (I even came out for Bernie Sanders a bunch of years ago, partly because I didn't know better back then.)

Even so, as a result of articulating my true beliefs now, and even with the success I've been blessed to have so far and the platforms I have today (which I've worked very, very hard for), I'm blacklisted today from many events.

Liberals don't want me among them or with them. As just one example, *Rolling Stone* magazine told a member of my team a few years ago that the publication flat-out wouldn't write about me anymore. This is ridiculous, of course, since I'm a musician and a creative person who is contributing regularly to the entertainment scene.

Isn't a publication like that *supposed to be* covering pop culture? Hmmm …

And this is what I'm saying. We've got to question things like this.

Stand up to it. #WalkAway from it because it's unfair, unjust, and *doesn't make sense.*

Proud to Make This Count

No matter what others choose to do, which I cannot control, this is all about communication for me. I love doing what I do. I love my work as a musician and a writer and an entertainer and a speaker.

I love communicating with people in so many ways about what I believe, who I am, and what I care about. I love communicating with all of you!

As a kickass conservative, I see myself as a voice for this generation.

I'm putting my values above self-gain.

I'm proud to make this count.

Legendary actor Isaiah Washington, whom I'm blessed to have as a friend, tweeted something on April 1, 2019, that explained why he, too, was leaving the Democratic Party behind after spending years among those on the left.

I'd been introduced to Isaiah by our mutual friend Brandon Straka. And his story is instructive.

Isaiah wrote, "I voted for 44 [Obama] twice. I even checked my emails in his Senate Office while lobbying for Salone to be given another chance to rebrand. Not once in 8 years was I given any support regarding Africa or the Black Agenda, but 45 invites me to the WH to celebrate the #FirstStepAct." (See his tweet below.)

Isaiah has been working in Hollywood for a very long time. He's famous for being on "Grey's Anatomy," as well as on many other TV shows and

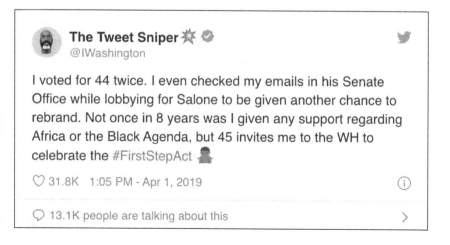

The Tweet Sniper ✅
@IWashington

I voted for 44 twice. I even checked my emails in his Senate Office while lobbying for Salone to be given another chance to rebrand. Not once in 8 years was I given any support regarding Africa or the Black Agenda, but 45 invites me to the WH to celebrate the #FirstStepAct 🗿

♡ 31.8K   1:05 PM - Apr 1, 2019   ⓘ

💬 13.1K people are talking about this   >

films. He's been around the block, has basically been an independent free thinker for years, and he's come out and said he's not afraid anymore.

He's been blacklisted for saying things and being outspoken in the past.

The bottom line is that this man is a fighter. And if you hadn't known what he looks like before now—not that it matters much—it *is* going to matter in this political context: He's Black.

Because of this, in the minds of many people, he and I and so many others don't fit the physical profile that society has "created" for conservatives or independents or for anyone outside of the Democrat Party. We, along with other conservative, libertarian, and independent creators, live in the Los Angeles area and work in Hollywood—so in a liberal-leaning town, that makes us "misfits." Ridiculous!

Fearless Honesty

Both Isaiah and I spoke at #WalkAway's Los Angeles Black Americans event in 2018, which featured other prominent conservative activists and voices.

At that event, I shared my own transformation of becoming a proud Trumplican and voting Trump into the White House in November 2016.

As an entertainer, an artist, and an activist, how do I stay so bold?

Fearless honesty helps me stay energized and creative.

I don't insult the work of other creative people. I can admire their creative paths, their work ethic, and their projects and creations even if their politics are different than mine.

And I would like them to do the same for me.

As they should.

Remember how actress Deborah Messing, who starred in the hit NBC sitcom "Will and Grace," tweeted out a message last year that anyone in Hollywood who attended a Beverly Hills Trump campaign fundraiser should be "outed" and put on a Hollywood blacklist?

Her tweet and her comments earned her a ton of backlash.

Even President Trump called her out for it.

Not that I like to give any more attention here than I need to, but I want you to see the hatred hidden in plain sight.

Here's her tweet:

Debra Messing ✓
@DebraMessing

Please print a list of all attendees please. The public has a right to know. twitter.com/THR/status/116...

The Hollywood Reporter ✓ @THR
President Donald Trump to appear at Beverly Hills fundraiser during Emmys week thr.cm/CgDyPb

♡ 79K   12:41 AM - Aug 31, 2019

💬 43.1K people are talking about this

Trump, of course, responded. (He never backs down—he fights for America and our ideals always!)

Here's what he tweeted:

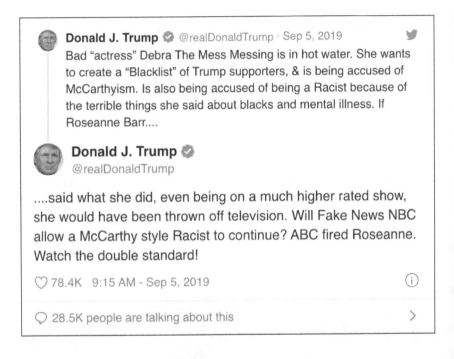

Donald J. Trump ✔ @realDonaldTrump · Sep 5, 2019

Bad "actress" Debra The Mess Messing is in hot water. She wants to create a "Blacklist" of Trump supporters, & is being accused of McCarthyism. Is also being accused of being a Racist because of the terrible things she said about blacks and mental illness. If Roseanne Barr....

Donald J. Trump ✔
@realDonaldTrump

....said what she did, even being on a much higher rated show, she would have been thrown off television. Will Fake News NBC allow a McCarthy style Racist to continue? ABC fired Roseanne. Watch the double standard!

♡ 78.4K   9:15 AM - Sep 5, 2019   ⓘ

💬 28.5K people are talking about this   〉

With all of this, it feels as if we tore an ugly page from Hollywood history back in the McCarthy era, when people suspected of communism were banned from working, creating, and speaking up. Has America now become the new Nazi Germany because of liberals like this?

But Hollywood won't be able to survive without conservatives. There are conservative producers on the music and business sides, and I know this because I've worked with them.

And now that I'm an outspoken conservative, they feel comfortable approaching me with an important admission.

It goes something like this: "I secretly support Trump. I support the president and what he's doing—but I'd be fired from [NBC, ABC, Paramount, you name it] if I say so publicly. So I'm telling you this privately."

There it is!

Be Forthright

Why aren't others speaking up? Why aren't they speaking out about their true feelings and beliefs?

You might be thinking, "But Joy! You can't tell people to do that in today's environment. They might lose their jobs."

Everyone must do what they feel is right—though if they're closeted in their beliefs, I hope they come out of that closet immediately!

I'm mostly addressing this to influential individuals. They should speak up about their beliefs, be honest about them, and be forthright during their time on this planet. They'll help not just Hollywood, but all of America.

They'll help *all of us*, no matter where we are or who we are.

Let's be truthful with each other.

Everyone has a voice and the ability to express it—and *should* have that right.

We can agree to disagree, but we must never take actions to silence one another.

Our country was built on freedom and that's what separates us from fascist and communist regimes.

My response to my liberal industry peers who try to silence others is this: You're allowed to be outspoken and political. But your beliefs mean nothing if you can't stand to see people who think differently than you have their voice and their choice.

You're masquerading as somebody who supports free speech if you yourself are trying to shut it down.

Calling Out the Idiots

The haters are everywhere, sadly. I'm going to lay it on the line here. They sneak into your DMS to tell you that you're wrong or that your last post was stupid.

They snub their nose at your jokes and chortle at your clothing changes.

They put down your attempts to be different, pooh-pooh your desires to explore something new, and sarcastically laugh at your expense when you attempt something that they didn't expect you to do.

They're idiots, but that doesn't mean their words and actions don't hurt.

It's anxiety-inducing enough in the world of entertainment and pop culture to put yourself out there or to try anything new. But when the threat of keyboard warriors looms—well, no wonder 50 percent of all new endeavors fail within the first three weeks.

So what do you do when the peanut gallery decides to chip in their two cents at your expense? (It's never dollars and actual sense, I might add.)

Let me indulge you with a little secret: *Everyone who does anything worthwhile is going to have haters!*

NOW, HERE'S MY REAL-LIFE TIP FOR YOU for dealing with the haters: If someone around you tells you, "I don't know if that's a good idea," or, "You should play it safer," it's a good bet that this person—who may be trying to "help" you for your "own good"—is certainly not out for your own good!

If it's from someone you care about, you should simply correct the person and say, "Thanks, but I'm going to do what's right for me. Don't worry. I've got this."

Shut down the person's advice immediately without deflating his or her entire balloon. And make sure you don't continue to listen to the person's criticism. Remarks like that can wear you down and make you doubt yourself.

The second type of criticism can be extremely negative and may come from someone who is *not* close to you. This type of hater is too afraid to actually confront you and may pretend that he or she knows you well—when, in fact, the person is a total stranger and doesn't know all the bold and admirable things you've done in your life, doesn't know the background, doesn't know how hard you've fought for yourself for years, and so much more.

When you encounter this snake in the grass, tell this person, "No, thank you," and walk away.

These people may appear out of nowhere—in social circles, on social media, in your work environment—to tell you how they feel about you or your actions.

Don't be misled.

They're not your friends!

The third and most aggressive form of criticism comes from the trolls and idiots online who attack you personally at all hours of the day and night. These maggots want to bring down others because the successful efforts of other people scare them to death. (I'm calling them out for what they are.)

For these people, the success of others puts fear and terror in their pea brains. Why? (I know—it's a weird thing to be afraid of, when you really think about it.)

But to see it from their perspective, these people fear anything better because they think it could "destroy" them.

I want you to get this into your glorious, incredibly intelligent heads: Haters are jealous of those of us who are trying to accomplish things, create things, and put new things into the world that weren't there before. They're jealous of other people's wins, successes, and triumphs, *period.*

And I'll tell you something from my own experience here: No hater ever bought my products or contributed anything positive or useful to my life.

So here's what I want to say directly to them: If you aren't paying my bills, then miss me with that dumb s***!

These people are useless as long as you never believe a word they say. Simply block them, mute them, unfriend them—and go about your business.

I believe in helping others grow with positive reinforcement. I work hard to stay upbeat and positive, and to buck the negative vibes that are out there. I welcome a range of voices in this world.

I'm very pragmatic. I believe that constructive criticism, when solicited from trustworthy people, can be a useful tool for bettering oneself. I am generally more open in this regard than many other people are, and I've worked hard to be this way. I'm proud of the way I am.

So I say to you if you encounter the haters: *Just keep going!*

And keep a healthy group of great family and friends around you to remind you of how extraordinary you are.

How special. How creative. How beautiful.

Don't buy into any or all of the negative waves out there.

Stay positive.

Listen to your own voice.

Trust yourself and your good, smart, amazing instincts!

CHAPTER 4

Why I'm Proudly Pro-Life and Always Will Be

The Pregnancy and Adoption That Changed Me Forever

"Life is the most precious, sacred gift we have been given."
—Abby Johnson

MY STATEMENT FOR THE 60th Grammys in early 2018 was "Choose Life," as I noted earlier. On the red carpet for that event (and as a follow-up to the first time I came out for Trump in early 2017), I wore a white gown by bridal designer Pronovias.

And on the full ball skirt, I handpainted an image based on the way my very own child looked in her sonogram when I was eight months pregnant with her. Around her image, I painted a rainbow.

A lot of people didn't know that the image was a near-reproduction of my very own baby. They soon found out, though!

Then, in 2019, I wore a provocative, pink latex gown to the Los Angeles premiere of the amazing film *Unplanned*, which was based on the book of the same name by Abby Johnson.

She had been a Planned Parenthood clinic worker in Texas but wisely (and dramatically) left that wretched group behind—and became a pro-life activist.

I called the pink latex gown my "Pro-Life Barbie" look, with of course a proudly rebellious message: "F*** Planned Parenthood."

As you can imagine, the critics *looooved* it!

I received thousands of rape threats and vile comments from people, many of them young teen girls, saying they hoped I'd get raped and die. Brainwashing by celebrities (and as funded by Planned Parenthood) has been abhorrently destructive to our teenage girls.

I also received thousands of supportive comments and letters, many of these from women and girls who were now choosing life over death.

My dress ultimately gave the middle finger to Planned Parenthood and to all the radical liberals who keep talking endlessly about being "pro-choice." What they're really saying is that they're "pro-abortion"—let's be honest about it. They're in favor of taking human life when that human life somehow becomes "inconvenient" for them.

I was standing up for life in the most public way I could, at a time when I had the most eyes on me. I did all of this pro-life messaging very deliberately. I wanted to showcase love. And I chose a very personal message to do that.

I wanted to shine a bright light on something that celebrities rarely discuss today. We almost never see pro-life issues talked about in public like this, unless we're at rallies or events specifically organized around these issues.

I believe in loving the child and the mother, and I am proudly pro-life, without any judgment of others.

And *why*, you ask, did I wear a painting of a fetus surrounded by a brightly colored womb on my dress and a purse that said "Choose Life" to the 60th Grammy Awards?

At the 2018 Grammy Awards, I wore a near-reproduction of my very own child on my dress.

Why did I slam Planned Parenthood so hard and so publicly?

More than a decade ago, my own life was shattered.

I couldn't stop crying.

I learned that I had a crisis pregnancy.

I learned that I had a beautiful baby growing inside of me. (I shared some of these details in an op-ed I wrote that was published by the Fox News website not long ago.)

So Young, So Afraid

For many women in stable, loving relationships, or many women of a certain age or circumstance, becoming pregnant can be, and is, a dream come true.

But when it happened to me back then, I was at first overcome with guilt, agony, and shame.

I mean, I was so young!

At age 19, I had fallen in love with an older man who was very kind-hearted. But once he began using drugs, our relationship quickly became a nightmare for me.

The same arms that once held and protected me were weaponized. Night after night, I'd hide in a corner, terrified of being beaten.

In those very dark, hard times, I didn't know where to turn.

And I was penniless, far from home, and trapped in a toxic relationship with someone who had become a shadow of what he once was.

Scary?

You bet.

When you're young and vulnerable, sometimes your mind plays tricks on you. You think, *I don't deserve happiness!*

You think, *I don't deserve love,* or, *I guess this is the best I can do.*

It pains me to remember how utterly devoid of value I felt all those years ago.

It is not at all how I feel today.

But for a while there, I truly believed that I deserved to be abandoned, forgotten, and punished. I thought, *This must be my fault, so I have to stay and try to fix this.*

I had—*still have!*—a stubborn streak in me. And I believed that once I started something, I had to stay the course—had to figure it out on my own, had to make it work.

After a contraceptive failed, I became pregnant at the age of 20.

I went to a local clinic to get a pregnancy test.

And when the pregnancy test came back positive, the nurse immediately began to pressure me to get an abortion—right then and there at the clinic.

That day.

She told me, "We can do it now. It's easy. It's free! It'll make it all go away."

She also revealed that she herself had had not one abortion, but *several* abortions.

"In fact, all three of my daughters have had several," this woman said to me. "You are too young to have children. This is the best choice for you."

So let's get this straight.

This nurse, a complete stranger to me—and someone who worked at the clinic for a living—*was trying to make my choice for me.* Yet she had no idea who I was, didn't know about my life, my beliefs, my heart, my head, my soul.

Well, guess what?

I wasn't buying what she was selling.

I told that nurse, "No."

And I walked right out of that clinic.

I was scared to death—shaking, upset, distraught.

But no one was going to tell me what to do with my very own baby.

You got that right, baby!

Had to Make It Better

I know what I'm talking about when I discuss pro-life issues, as I said in an interview with Jesse Lee Peterson on his TV show, "The Fallen State." My heart breaks for the unborn and at the horrors and flat-out lies of Planned Parenthood.

Abortion is not health care. Babies are living things!

They're human beings, not clumps of fetal tissue.

Think about it: *No parent ever mourned the miscarriage of a "clump of fetal tissue."*

I had never considered abortion.

I believed in life.

I wanted to stay and make things right with the baby's father, to have a real family. I thought that's what I should do.

And I remained shocked and upset that at the very moment I learned I was pregnant with a child, a clinic worker tried to talk me into an abortion as a way of "making it all go away."

I'll say it again: *I believe in life.*

I prayed to God constantly.

I knew I was in a bad situation and that I had to make it better somehow.

Then one day, when I was violently thrown against the wall while I was much further along in my pregnancy, I knew I needed a real solution.

I knew I had to take some dramatic action.

I left to be on my own.

My baby deserved so much better.

And that's when God gave me the idea of adoption.

A lot of people don't know all of this about me. I'm sharing my story very honestly so that all of you know where I'm coming from on the pro-life issue.

My beliefs are heartfelt and from my soul.

And perhaps in some way, my personal story might help you or others close to you face whatever circumstances or challenges you're dealing with in your own lives. That is my fervent prayer.

Anyway, I looked down at the table where I was sitting at that moment, and there was a newspaper. It was lying open.

And an article in it said, "Loving homes looking to adopt."

That's when I made the most difficult and important decision of my young life. I decided I would carry my baby to full term on my own.

I would give her the life she completely deserved—and then try to adopt her out to a beautiful, loving, kind, and generous family.

I chose to put her life over mine.

It was one of the hardest things I have *ever* done.

Every single day was a struggle. But it was the right thing to do.

You know what? I would do it again in a heartbeat—*because of my own baby's heartbeat.*

'Growing' Another Human Being

Pregnancy is extraordinarily difficult, especially without any family by your side. The mother's body is growing and changing every day as the child inside her grows.

The way you walk changes over time; the way you breathe changes; the way you sleep changes; the way you interact with the world changes.

Your body is growing and nurturing another human being.

Not only that, your entire conception of who you are as a human being and what your future may hold is changing, too.

I stayed with my dad for a big chunk of my pregnancy while missing my mom intensely—by this time, she'd suffered a stroke and had passed away after being in a coma for three days. It was a time of tremendous upheaval in my life. (I share more about all of this later in the book, including how I arrived at my JoyTribe mindset.)

Mostly I was by myself, thinking, planning, and trying to stay healthy for my baby. And my faith in God and my love for my growing baby gave me the strength I needed to survive. I kept asking God to guide me.

And He did!

And here's what you need to know about me as a conservative, because this may help you grow in your own journey. As a proud conservative, I believe in the right to life that all human beings possess—that we are given a gift by Our Creator to live and survive from womb to tomb.

And I believe in the family unit—that it is the backbone of society and should be protected, respected, and honored. And that fighting for our individual freedoms is the most important fight because it protects our past, present, and future generations.

Adoption is an important option that's being left out of the pro-life, pro-choice argument today.

It should not be left out.

It should be *prominent* in these discussions.

I made the decision for life and I will stand behind it forever.

My baby deserved everything.

My child was a gift from God.

Loving, Caring Family

I wanted my child to have the best life possible. And when my beautiful baby girl was finally born, I looked into her sweet, adorable face and renewed my commitment to myself and to her to do the very best thing I could for her.

Life is a gift! And "every person is worth protecting," as President Trump said.

I found an adoption agency that helped me every step of the way, including taking care of my day-to-day living expenses. And I placed my baby with a loving, caring family in an open adoption, which meant I could still be involved in her life.

Forever and always, I love her with all my heart.

I am able to see her. And I continue, to this very day, to have a growing and wonderful relationship with my daughter, who calls me "Mama Joy" because of my decision to choose life.

(I keep most of these details private, for her sake, as I'm sure you've figured out by now. She deserves to live her wonderful life in peace and privacy.)

Life Matters Most

The adoption route gave me—as a terrified young teenager who found herself pregnant by mistake—the greatest gift of her life.

It gave me a second chance, a chance to do the right thing, a chance at healing, and a chance to be a mom, even if I wasn't going to be the actual hands-on mom of this child.

So yes, in 2018 at the Grammys, I was celebrating my beautiful daughter by handpainting my gown with a recreation of my own child's sonogram. I didn't care what people said about me or about what I wore or did.

I was proud to do it. *It's life that matters most.*

I knew the baby I had carried. I knew her intimately.

No one else did!

And this is another reason I support President Trump. He is firmly, unabashedly, enthusiastically pro-life.

Thank God for our country's fearless leader!

In January of this year (again, our pre-COVID times seem *soooo* long ago as I write this), Trump became the first U.S. president to attend the

March for Life in Washington, D.C. This annual anti-abortion event is so important to all those of us who stand for life.

At the gathering this year, Trump didn't hold back, calling out those on the left for their "radical and extreme positions" on abortion. And he heaped praise on all those who attended the event in the nation's capital, noting that these individuals were and are filled with "pure, unselfish love."

"Unborn children have never had a stronger defender in the White House," Trump also said. "Every life brings love into this world. Every child brings joy to a family. Every person is worth protecting," he said.

God bless our president!

Consider Adoption

Today, I encourage women to think for themselves and to gather all the information they possibly can before making their own decision about their pregnancy.

Having life-giving and life-saving options such as adoption can em-power women to do what *they* feel is right—not what other people may think is "right."

Thousands of women at this very moment are in situations similar to the one I was in more than a decade ago. And many women and girls are even younger and far more vulnerable than I was at the time.

I'm not here to condemn anyone. I'm not calling anyone names or try-ing to make vulnerable young women feel worse than they might already do, from all the other things other people have told them or from what society suggests. There's already too much negativity in the world.

(And liberals think that young women can just wipe away a "problem pregnancy" by eliminating it—by killing it, doing away with it. *Ugh!*)

I do have a message—a strong and passionate plea for young women who might find themselves pregnant when they didn't expect to be.

Consider adoption for your baby.

Please consider life.

Please consider carrying your innocent little baby to term and placing your child with a caring, happy family that will give your newborn all the love, attention, and resources your sweet child deserves.

You *will* make it through this experience.

You deserve all the happiness and love in the world!

You're so much stronger than you know.

You deserve a second chance at life—and your baby deserves a *first* chance.

Life is precious.

And so are you!

My Testimony

I am a woman who's not ashamed to talk about pro-life values in such a public way. I chose life over death for my own child. And I choose life over death every day of my life.

I'm outspoken about it, and I'm an activist for life *forever.*

I have talked about this in many interviews, and I'll continue to speak out on the subject. You won't find many celebrities who are doing this.

I don't care about that. I care about speaking my beliefs.

I have no regrets. The person I am today is based on the choices I made yesterday—and my past is part of my life, my present, and my future. It's my testimony.

Being a pro-life advocate is something very personal and something that should be done in love. It shouldn't be political. Yet for some reason, too many people try to twist this topic, usually for their own ends.

I get a lot of negativity about being pro-life. (Yep, it's all those haters again. They're always out there.)

And that just shows the hypocrisy of the other side—of liberals, of liberalism, of the left.

Here I am, a strong woman, a woman of color, a conservative woman who's sharing my beliefs, yet the other side tries to shut me down.

Ironic, right?

When I was at the One Life March in downtown Los Angeles a few years ago—the pro-life event that celebrates the beauty and dignity of every human life—it coincided with the Women's March. And many of the Women's March folks who were out there were so nasty.

They were screaming and yelling at me, telling me I had no right to decide in favor of life. There were a lot of men screaming at me, too, about this.

It's kind of crazy that even now in our country, in 2020, we have to defend our beliefs. We have to fight for our right-to-life positions.

But it's all true.

And knowing this, and knowing what we're up against, gives us power.

NOW, HERE'S MY REAL-LIFE TIP FOR YOU for being pro-life in 2020 and beyond: In your own personal circles, articulate what you truly and authentically believe.

Don't allow anyone to talk you out of your own beliefs.

Don't allow anyone to sway you.

If you're a young conservative who believes in life and who believes in the right to life, speak up about it! And join with others who believe this, too. (My recommended reading list at the back of this book will help. You'll see pro-life resources there.)

There are plenty of us out here.

Others can believe what they want (although how anyone can go against innocent life created and blessed by God is beyond me)—but your beliefs are *yours*.

If you fervently, passionately, and wholeheartedly believe that life begins at conception, as I do and as so many millions of other pro-life Americans do, share those beliefs with those around you *and do everything you can to live them out.*

Most of all, do not allow anyone to talk you into anything, including abortion, if it goes against your most sacred and heart-directed beliefs.

Connect with others who believe in life.

Take a breath. Pause. Think.

Ask for more information if you need it. Ask for help if you need it.

If you're a young woman who finds herself pregnant, please know and remember that *abortion is not your only choice,* as too many clinics would have you believe. And that the precious life you're carrying within you deserves a chance.

Life is bigger and far more important.

Pregnancy resource centers (PRC) around the country—and there is probably one, or maybe more, near you—are nonprofit groups that help women find alternatives to abortion. Many women choose life for their unborn babies after they visit one of these centers. You can, too!

Call the free 24/7 service Option Line at 800-712-HELP (800-712-4357). It can refer you to a PRC in your area so that you can get help in person. Or visit www.optionline.org. (I'm sharing info as posted by Focus on the Family.)

Many other terrific organizations actively promote pro-life values. There are literally hundreds of national and local pro-life groups that can share information and advice—as well as opportunities for activism, if that's your choice.

So please reach out.

Ask a trusted family member, a friend, a colleague, a neighbor for help. And don't be embarrassed or ashamed! You're carrying human life and it's worth protecting.

You can look locally first or reach out to the biggest national pro-life groups as well. Most of them have established local chapters. And please, again, see the resources for conservatives at the back of the book.

Most of all, *act on your own beliefs.*

Believe in yourself and your values.

Trust your heart.

Trust yourself.

And know that you are not alone! *You can do this.*

I know because I was there myself.

And today my child is *alive.*

CHAPTER 5

I'm Feminine, Not Feminist

How I Rejected Feminism to Find
My True Girl Power

"I defy gravity." —Marilyn Monroe

I WANT TO TALK to you now about a very popular but not-nearly-as-fun word as my other favorite F-word: feminism. I'm not just speaking to women. This is for the dudes, too.

As I set my sights on being an even stronger and better woman than I've been before, the title of feminism no longer serves me.

This is a big part of my life today as a conservative. It might be part of yours, too.

As a little girl, I distinctly remember looking up to the strong women in my life. My aunt was a captain in the Marines. My mother battled mental illness her whole life—yet, as a stay-at-home mom, she woke up every day to take care of her three children. She also provided for her family as a fiber artist who created beautiful rugs, paintings, and artwork.

My mom found the time to laugh, dance, and create music on her guitar and piano for church. She made our home a really special place for

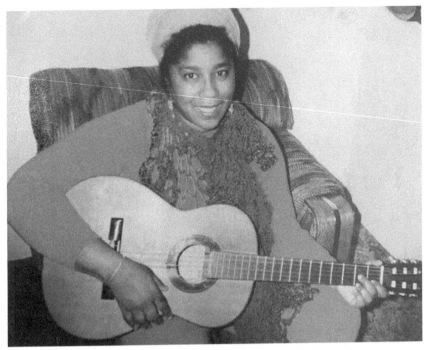

My talented mom in the 1990s. Playing guitar always soothed her mind.

me, my dad, and my siblings. These are the strong women I looked up to in my life. My mom, a pastor's wife, was sweet and always hugged me. She was the epitome of feminine energy. She held me in her arms and enveloped me with warmth and love.

She had the strength and the ability to be soft and vulnerable. Yet she was also hard and determined to have the hustle, yet not be a hustler.

She could be a tough woman, but she also let others see the little girl inside of that.

That's how I've been able to be a strong woman in my own life—to fight for the rights of others, female and male. To stand up for values and principles. And to stand up for life, for the unborn and the born.

I was raised with that belief, that this is what makes a strong woman.

Nerdy Girl and Proud of It

I also looked up to Mae Jemison, the first Black female astronaut. In 1992, Jemison flew aboard the space shuttle Endeavour for NASA, becoming the first African-American woman in space. I looked up to other iconic Black women as well, but NASA's Mae Jemison was my favorite.

Maybe that could be me one day, I thought, as a nerdy girl who loved space, travel, and science.

I found out about her in a book of historic Black women. And Rosa Parks—I looked up to Rosa Parks for her fight for equality for all people.

My mom used to say Rosa's feet were tired, and that's what started the entire Montgomery bus boycott in 1955 and everything else that followed.

These were the epitome of strong women for me. I never had the idea that because I was a female, I couldn't accomplish my dreams and goals due to the gender of my body. I never believed that. I was never taught that.

Also, I was not raised to value my physical beauty as a tool or an asset to get me the job I wanted. Neither was I raised to *devalue* my physical gender as something that wouldn't give me the job I wanted.

I looked at things with my mind and my heart, with my creativity and my soul. And I thought about how much I could achieve in life if I worked really, really hard. These were the ideas that occupied my young mind.

They still occupy my mind today.

These are the things that made me who I am, knowing that I could do all things through Christ, who strengthens me—as my father, a preacher, would often tell me.

Biggest Cheerleader

I knew that I was created to shine a light for others, to be the light that would shine inwardly as well, to be my own biggest cheerleader.

And I felt that I could accomplish anything I set my mind to; even as a little girl I felt this way. I knew I would do big things, and I knew I would accomplish great goals.

I knew I would be famous, wealthy, and well-loved—not because those things individually mean anything, but because those things, taken together, could help me create the positive, glowing, and beautiful manifestation of a life well-lived.

I knew I had the ability to touch others with my voice, with my dreams, and with my goals—and that I'd be able to encourage people and touch something deep inside them that is spiritual.

This is why I'm telling you now, as I've said before: Yes, you are a spiritual being. You can dictate your life as you choose. You can write your story.

And you're not just the actor in this story. You're the director, the producer, and the cinematographer of the beautiful cinematic film that is your own life.

This is what I tell my JoyTribe all the time.

And this is how I created the version of myself that you see today, someone who is the most authentic woman I've ever been. In fact, I'm now the woman I've always wanted to know! I am the woman I wanted to see when I felt young and beautiful on the inside but vulnerable on the outside.

Years ago, it was nothing but a dream when I was young.

Now, this is my reality.

And I'm no longer a feminist.

I actually reject the title of feminist.

I *reject* the whole notion of raging feminism.

Why, you ask?

Let me tell you!

All Shapes and Sizes

It's not because I'm not "pro the vote," or not in favor of a woman's right to command what she does with her body—and by this I mean her own body, not the body of a child that may be living inside her, who is another being entirely.

I'm saying I believe that women should be able to get tattoos or wear skimpy clothes if they wish. They can wear long dresses to cover up, or they can show off all the hard work they're doing to stay healthy and fit.

I believe that women come in all shapes and sizes, and all of them are beautiful.

As long as we're healthy, we women can be tall, short, round, have a few extra pounds, or maybe even be a little underweight—and still be beautiful.

I believe that women can be whoever we want to be.

But today's feminism—the feminism of the left—insists that women must *reject* the world of men. Today's feminism says that women are *less* than men. It says that what's between our legs must dictate how women think, how we vote, and what we do. This is ridiculous.

It says that we should vote for another individual simply because that person has the same anatomy as we do, never mind if her values are different from our own.

How crazy is that?

Feminism told me, when I was a young actress just starting out, that if I didn't preach feminism to the masses like I was in some sick, ritualistic cult, then I didn't count as a woman, that I wasn't helping my fellow women.

Feminism told me that I wouldn't be able to achieve my goals because of the body I happened to be born into.

Feminism *didn't* tell me that if I worked hard, treated others with respect, and kept going after my goals, I would achieve them.

No! Today's leftist feminism tells women that there's this huge entity lurking like a demon in our lives, hidden in the shadows, a monster hiding under the bed. It says it will snatch our dreams away.

What is this demon?

It's called *the patriarchy*.

What a big, scary word—"patriarchy."

Ooh. Five points at least!

To feminists today, patriarchy means that male-dominated systems control women. It means that we can't achieve our goals unless we band together, take off our tops, go braless, and march side by side in the Women's March.

Unless I use the required hashtags, this doctrine demands, then I'm not really a woman at all.

For years I drank the Kool-Aid of feminism. For years I believed that the louder I shouted for women's rights, the more rights that women would have—instead of opening my eyes and awakening to the fact that in this day and age, *women in the West already have more rights than ever before.*

What Real Women Know

If you are blessed enough to be born in America, or if you've been able to immigrate here legally, you have absolute equal rights as a female.

I had to do my own research to debunk the wage-gap nonsense that you often hear in the liberal media, by the way. I used my intelligence, not just my emotions, to see that women take lower paying jobs or work fewer hours selectively because—as women, as moms, as females—we care about others.

We nurture others.

We value ourselves.

We #self-care on a daily basis.

Most men do not!

That's why women tend to live longer than men.

Most women know how to de-stress and talk about our problems and issues. We talk about our feelings. We talk about our emotions, which are incredible. I don't have a problem acknowledging and using my feelings and emotions. But I do have a problem with a political system that tells me I must allow those feelings and emotions to *dictate how I vote*—and that only feelings and emotions matter.

Not logic.

Not thinking.

Not intelligence.

Not reasoning.

And I'm going to toot my own horn here for a moment. I'm a very intelligent woman. Most people don't see that coming.

They see the packaging, which is pretty. I work hard for the body I have, for the fitness level I have, for the good health I enjoy. And I share a lot of the details of that with my JoyTribe regularly (and in this book, too).

I'm a vegan and have been a vegan for 16 years. I work out for an hour every day, five days a week.

I take my vitamins. I have a cruelty-free skincare regimen. I get eight-plus hours of sleep every night.

And I do all of this because it's my job to take care of myself so that I can stay healthy enough to provide content for my followers, to support myself, and to provide for my future family.

I'm a woman who takes care of my community and those around me, male and female.

And now that I've rejected the title of feminism and all of its restraints and restrictions, I'm not afraid to do this.

And I love the man I'm with, and I'll continue to nurture him and push him forward while also nurturing and pushing myself forward.

joyvilla ✔ • Following
Los Angeles, California

joyvilla ✔ #joytribe Can I just brag on this beautiful man, Ryan, real quick? 5 months together, which feels so comfortable, well aligned and soooo good. 💜 He makes me glow, laugh, smile, and yes often roll my eyes! 🙄 I've cried in his arms multiple times, been a mess sometimes, let my "tough girl" shield down and showed him my vulnerability when it scared me to do so....he didn't run. He didn't taunt. He just comforted me. He's not only gorgeous and strong of body, but brilliant of mind in parts I struggle with as a wild artist. He's logical, compassionate, kind, a great communicator and the amazing love of my life. 💜 💍 👰 Baby, I cant believe it's only been 5

85 likes

2 MINUTES AGO

Add a comment...

(Here's my Instagram post about my beloved Ryan!)

I'm not afraid to be vulnerable, to be soft, and to cry in front of others, including the man I love.

Yet I'm stronger and better because I let these womanly feelings show!

Shocking, right?

I guarantee you that today's feminism will never tell you this.

The Cringy T-Shirts I Once Wore

Yep. Feminism told me to "never let them see you cry"—that you must be a tough girl.

This makes me recall the T-shirts I used to wear as a feminist years ago—and I laugh. I hope you'll laugh at them, too (though some of my more delicate readers may be offended by some of these slogans).

I was cleaning out my closet recently (as my boyfriend will attest, there were a bazillion old costumes and clothes!). As I sipped my matcha tea for energy and blasted David Bowie, I stumbled upon some of the wild things I used to wear in my "previous life."

Some of it was from my sex, drugs, and rock 'n' roll days—the kinky affects and all. And I'm being very honest about my past. I'm not afraid of it. I've grown because of it. I've grown *from* it. (You'll see more detail on this later in the book.) I used to wear things that would shock your grandma, your mom, and *you!*

Anyway, as I pushed through the bullet bras, the spikey corsets, the latex dresses, and all the other sexy getups I used to wear, the most shocking things I found were some T-shirts. I distinctly remember getting one of these shirts back in 2012 in San Francisco while I was on a tour stop.

This T-shirt said, "When God made man, She was only joking."

Another shirt that I ordered online at a funky, artsy boutique—thinking, "This will show 'em who I am! This will prove who I am!"—said, "Real women intimidate boys and excite men."

In and of themselves, these slogans are harmless. I also wore them with a bit of irony and a crooked smile, you know?

But I felt an intrinsic need back then to push the idea that women must be strong, must be superior, that women will rule the world.

In reality, that wasn't how I truly felt.

I didn't hate men at all. I was in love with and married to a man at that time! What the feminists were pushing and are still pushing is not equality. It's domination.

Nope, Can't Say That

As I share all of this with you, I also want to say that third-wave feminism has done more harm for young girls than liberals will ever admit.

It's confused single women and thrown more men into a tizzy than ever before—along with the #MeToo movement, which has practically *destroyed* dating.

Today, nobody can touch anybody for fear of being reported or for fear of sexual harassment—even when it's gentle and well-intentioned.

A man can't say to a woman, "Hey, you look pretty."

No! That's sexist, according to leftist feminism.

And no man can *ever* compliment a little girl on her looks.

It is usually a very innocent thing to say, "Oh, what a pretty baby she is!" Or, "What a beautiful young girl," or, "You're beautiful," or, "Your hair looks good." (Unless the comment is coming from Joe Biden—*ugh*. But I digress!)

The truth is that women and girls give compliments to each other all the time. My girlfriends and I are always showering adoration and compliments on each other because *that's what girls do.*

That's what we love. That's *how* we love.

Women nurture. Women protect.

Men go after things. But women can also use masculine energy in their lives and still be feminine.

Once I rejected the label of feminism in my life, realizing it was doing nothing to help me, that's when I became feminine. I became soft. And yet I became stronger than ever before as I cracked the hard, outer shell of society's hold on me.

It's a Trap

As a young millennial woman of color in the creative and artistic scene in Hollywood, I finally realized that feminism was a trap.

It was even a type of bondage to a title and to a group that I had no connection with whatsoever.

In my career, no feminist has ever reached out to help me. No feminist has ever promoted my music or lent a helping hand. Feminists haven't pushed me to the top of the music charts.

Today's feminism has done nothing for me!

Sure, first-wave feminism told women that they were not the property of their husbands. That was true change; that was real justice.

And second-wave feminists fought for women to have the vote, to be seen as equal human beings in the eyes of the law.

Again, those women were true warriors.

Women are not the property of their husbands, just as husbands are not the property of their wives. Human beings should be independent individuals who choose to love someone, the person of their choice, with their God-given freedoms and rights.

Unfortunately, in most parts of the world, that's not a reality for many women. In America, it is. Yet in America, we have more loudmouthed, blue-haired, single, fat, and unhappy feminists than ever before!

It's true. And this is a tragedy.

We have more rights today than ever before—yet so many women are more unhappy. We have all the rights and all the unhappiness.

This is Netflix feminism. It's people sitting on their couches streaming a documentary and then going on Twitter and hashtagging the hell out of it.

That is what feminism has become today. It's a travesty.

It's "free the nipple" instead of "free the female" or "free the family"!

These people say, "Let's change the pronouns. And let's change how we spell 'women.' Let's put an X in there."

They're all about identity—instead of finding a true purpose and true identity in life, which exists not just for the "self" but for others around you, for your loved ones, for the communities you live and work in, for the values you hold dear, and for how you express those values.

These things make up what we are and who we are. Hashtags and "directions" from liberal segments of our society do not.

Yet that's what too many of our young people today have been brainwashed into believing.

Back in 2013, I hashtagged everything—I thought I was supposed to do it. I wore orange when it was supposed to be about fighting gun violence. I promoted female speakers because my peers on Facebook told me to do it. I wore feminist slogans and proudly called myself a feminist on social media for years.

I thought it was the right thing to do. I was young, ignorant, and naïve back then. I've grown—and I understand so much more now.

I'm a gun-toting, Second Amendment-supporting, right-lovin', NRA-belonging, feminine woman who has a successful career and hopes to start a family soon!

And through my actions today as a kickass conservative, I'm trying to help other young women grow and understand the strength they have within themselves.

Never Enough?

Right about now, you might be saying, "But Joy! Everything you've been saying is what feminism preaches."

Wrong!

Feminism may say, "We want equality. We want girls to be seen as equal to boys."

But the reality is that when we have it—which we do in America—it's never enough.

Now we want *female-led imperialism.*

Now, if we need more young women in the science or math fields, feminism says, "Let's overlook the male applicants and put women there instead."

They're fighting for the rights of women without asking those women what they really want.

Many women *want* to stay home and have babies. They *want* to be homemakers. They *want* to be at home with their children. And that's as much about being a strong female as it is about being a surgeon, or a lawyer, or a leading politician in Congress.

We need all types of women in all types of professions. We need stay-at-home moms. We need preachers, teachers, nurses, politicians, truck drivers, mathematicians, makeup artists, designers, performers, writers, and deep-sea divers.

Yes, we should not stop encouraging women to pursue their interests. But we should never make laws that say, "Every profession must be 50-50," or, "We must have equal numbers of men and women." By doing that, you're actually pushing women into fields that they may not even want to be part of—and pushing men *out* of these fields.

How is that fair?

And by the way, modern feminists really don't want to support the empowerment of women. If they did, they wouldn't be advocating against strong women who value their Second Amendment rights!

I agree that women shouldn't need saving. But if we're going to shake the damsel-in-distress stereotype, we need to learn how to save ourselves.

"Feminism" as we know it today needs to be redefined.

And I have the perfect word instead.

When I say I love and fight for women—and I want women to be stronger and better, and believe in themselves, and have happy families, happy bodies, happy spiritual lives, happy careers, happy lives—I am not a feminist.

Nope. I fully reject that title.

Instead, I am *pro-woman. And that doesn't mean I'm anti-man!*

NOW, HERE'S MY REAL-LIFE TIP FOR YOU for rejecting feminism in 2020 and beyond: When an "ism" such as this puts the identity of the group over the identities of the individuals involved—question it!

Step back. Take a moment before you join in.

Maybe it's not for you!

Understand that you can be "pro-woman" without embracing feminism.

Understand that you can be "pro-woman" without rejecting men.

Understand that you can be "pro-woman" without rejecting yourself.

And understand that being feminine today can include being as tough as nails, and as soft and sweet as a blanket. They are not mutually exclusive.

I say: Get involved in causes that you believe in 100 percent, not causes that you "think" you should support just because others around you (including on social media) say you should.

Again, we get one life here.

And in this one life, it's about being an individual, about using our own minds, our own judgment, and our own intelligence and reasoning to reach conclusions and make decisions.

And guess what?

It's OK to be "pro-woman" and to be a Trumplican.

It's OK to be "pro-woman" and a conservative.

They're not mutually exclusive, either.

How do I know that for sure?

Easy. I'm the kickass living proof!

CHAPTER 6

A Conservative Woman of Color in a Cancel Culture

You'll Never Believe What Someone Said to My Face

"Black supremacy is just as dangerous as White supremacy."
—Martin Luther King Jr.

MANY PEOPLE CALL ME "that young, Black, conservative singer who supports Trump." They use that description as either a plus or a minus, depending on their viewpoint.

Well, I *am* young, I *am* Black, I *am* conservative, I *am* a singer, and I *do* support Trump. So they've got all those individual parts right.

But there's so much more of my background and my beliefs that I want you to know, especially during this virulent time in our history, when an outrageous "cancel culture" has somehow become all the rage.

I'm sharing all of this with you—my JoyTribe and all of my readers—as a fervent, Trump-supporting conservative, and as someone who wants to help you in your own kickass journey.

I'm being authentic with you, one on one.

And I'm challenging the obnoxiousness and the outrageousness that's out there today. For years I've actually gotten this ignorant question thrown in my face: "What are you?"

I'm of mixed heritage and race.

I'm biracial.

And digging into my ancestry has brought up even more of my mixed-race heritage.

On my mom's side, I'm Black and Choctaw Native-American. And on my dad's side, I'm Italian and Argentinian.

I'm very proud to be Black. I serve on the Black Voices for Trump group, as I noted a bit earlier in this book. I also serve on the boards of different charities that help the Black community. I feel that this work is hugely important. It ties into conservative values.

Yes, I believe that we should have charities in our country, but these charities should be run by individuals and churches, not by the government. I do believe in social betterment programs 100 percent, but this work should not be left up to the government. Why? Because the government bungles things.

This always happens. The government mismanages funds.

I mean every word of this.

I'm also very proud to be Latina. And as a Latina, I'm a proud member of the White House National Hispanic Community group. I attend Hispanic Heritage Month events and am on regular phone calls with White House executives and with President Trump himself.

I'm proud of every part of my mixed background. It's helped shape my unique perspectives on politics, society, education, and Black and Latin American culture in this country.

And I want to talk about race relations in the U.S.A., because they've gotten so bad right now. They were bad under Obama, but this year, with everything that's been going on, they're *awful*.

And when I shared the Martin Luther King quote that starts this chapter, by the way—"Black supremacy is just as dangerous as White supremacy"—on Twitter and Instagram in early July of this year, it got a *ton* of attention and conversation.

People really reacted (over 8,000 likes on Instagram alone in three days) to my posting of something Dr. King said back in September of 1960.

My message when I posted it was this: Listen to the wise words of a man who sacrificed everything for *equality*, not *supremacy*. As a Black woman, I see the injustices done in my community, and yes, I want change. But this ain't the way!

The violence, the looting, the anger, the outrage—it's all tearing our country apart rather than building it, rather than putting it together, rather than moving it forward. Dr. King was so far ahead of his time that his words, unfortunately, are still needed today.

Have we learned nothing?

Well, let me tell me you something. Critics have often said to me, "You don't count as Black because you're mixed."

My whole life I've had to deal with this.

This is a very big part of my life as a conservative woman of color in today's America.

At the end of the day, we are all different colors in this country—and that makes us beautiful. We're all different colors, shapes, and sizes, and that's really important to acknowledge and appreciate.

It's not just our identity; it's about pride.

It's about standing up for ourselves and for what we are.

And it's about rejecting the ignorance, the intolerance, the discomfort, and the judgment that comes from too many people toward those of us who have the gall and the guts to be authentic and to think for ourselves.

Will I Be Safe?

When I began writing the first draft of this chapter, I was wearing a Trump tank top as I worked inside my home. And when I put my writing aside for a few moments to go for a walk, I actually had to think consciously before I stepped outside: *Should I leave my Trump shirt on when I go walking around the streets of Los Angeles? Or not?*

I wondered: *Will I be safe in the city if I leave this shirt on? Will anyone stop me or say anything (or worse) if they see me wearing this?*

Pray for me!

And then I pushed right back at those worries. My attitude was and is, I'm going to do it! This is America. This is what I'm wearing right now casually around my home—and there's nothing wrong with it. And, yep, even outside my home in Los Angeles, I'm going to wear it. OK? OK! (I did wear that tank top that day during a walk, and nothing happened to me, thank God. But look at all the unnecessary angst about this. *Crazy.*)

When I go to visit my family in D.C., in Virginia, and in New York, I wear things like this, too.

And on this very topic, I want to share what happened to me last year and how I was stopped because of something I wore that was pro-Trump. The incident went viral on Twitter when it happened last July, with the tweet video grabbing over two million-plus views. Clearly it struck a chord.

I was walking through Dulles International Airport in the D.C. area. I had just attended one of the White House events and had spoken at another event for a conservative group, about (ironically enough) the suppression of conservatives on social media.

When the event wrapped up, I didn't have time to change. So I went directly to the airport to fly home to Los Angeles (to see my cats!).

And I was wearing a small, glittery Trump pin, which was prominent on my clothing. As I walked through one of the main terminals, a White woman—an older woman with short, straight, gray hair—looked at me and gave me a hateful look. And she said to me as I walked by, "You're gross."

She basically spat out the words—looking directly into my face as she said them.

I turned red immediately. I did not feel safe, instantly, in that moment. It was horrible.

I felt her disgust and her anger coming at me like daggers.

I also felt shocked to my core that in these modern times, something like this would happen to me.

This, even after having a Black president in our country; even after having many civil rights cases pushed to court to help free Black Americans from an unjust prison system (and there's more work to be done on that); even after having a White president who signed the First Step Act—which was truly historic on the part of President Trump; and even after seeing so many Black and brown faces on television and all across our diversified, multi-racial, multi-cultural media.

Even with all of that, still, a White woman today would say directly to me, a Black woman, that I was "gross."

Unreal.

Had to Confront Her

My first thought was that I should ignore the comment. Just move on. I felt victimized in that moment. I knew I hadn't done anything wrong—other than exist.

And I felt that I shouldn't stir the pot, that what this woman said was wrong but that it was just the way things were and that I should let it go.

But *no!*

I had to confront her about it. What she said was so wrong on its face

Joy Villa

that I felt I had to speak to this person and push back. So I turned on my phone's videocamera and began recording.

I walked toward the woman, who was now standing in one place with her suitcase, and I said, "Excuse me, ma'am. What was that you said to me? What did you call me?"

And she said, lying right into my phone, "I said nothing."

I repeated, "What did you just say? Did you say I was 'gross'?"

She said, "I didn't like the pin. The pin is gross. Trump is gross."

I replied, "You didn't say that. You said, 'Gross.' You looked right in my face and said I was 'gross.'"

"Yeah, I meant the pin," she said.

As she began talking over me (and with that same contemptuous attitude), I said directly to her in a calm, even voice—and you can hear me say this on the video of our interaction—"Calling a woman 'gross' in a public place is not OK. You can disagree with someone's politics, but it's not OK to attack me and call me 'gross.'"

"I'm not attacking you," she said, a little louder now. "I said that about your Trump pin."

"You didn't say that," I responded to her. "I had to walk up and ask you again. I hope you learn some manners," I added. "Because you're not a young person anymore. You're a woman who's a grown adult. And that's not OK. To call somebody 'gross' in a public place—that's not polite."

She said, "Well, that's my choice. I called your pin gross."

By this point some people had seen us talking and began to look our way; there were witnesses around us. And I said to her, to make sure she got my drift, "Shame on you for trying to shame me."

That's the gist of what happened that day.

I felt that the entire thing was outrageous. I can support President Trump publicly in our country and I'm not going to be ashamed—as an

Afro-Latina woman—to do so in public. Why in today's climate does it seem OK to some people to treat another human being the way this woman treated me?

I wouldn't do that to another person.

During the Obama years, I know plenty of people, both Black and White, who wore Obama clothing or buttons or other gear during his presidency (and some still do). No one ever said a word to them or even *dared* to say a word.

Yet today, somehow it's a big problem if a Black woman—and a conservative woman (whether that individual who said "gross" to me knew that about me or not)—wears something in public in support of President Trump.

I'm assuming, because of her words and actions, by the way, that this older woman is a liberal, a member of the so-called "party of tolerance." And to her and others like her, I am going to emphasize this: It is never OK to mistreat somebody in this way. And it's unacceptable to me that actions like this (and so much worse) are becoming the norm toward conservatives of color or, frankly, toward anyone who dares in any way to depart from the liberal, leftist script.

I share what happened to me to illustrate that hate can come at you from all angles. That woman probably tells people that she's not racially motivated and that she would never be. Yet the fact is this: A White woman told a Black woman in America in 2019 that she's "gross" simply for wearing a pin in support of the president of the United States.

It happened. It's real. And it's reprehensible.

They Want Us to 'Choose' a Race

It used to be that 50 percent or so of the people in the country supported the president no matter what. With a 50-50 split, it's usually understood that, "Well, this individual is now our president, so we're going to respect the office and put up with it for the next four to eight years." But what's going on today is beyond anything I've ever seen.

Black Americans, Hispanic Americans, Asian Americans, and anyone else of any color, race, or ethnicity who supports President Trump are called vicious, nasty names and treated immorally by members of the so-called "tolerant left." We are seen as people who can no longer be "controlled." And that's exactly what the leftist mob wants today—control.

I've been told for years that I have to "choose" a race. I'm not White enough to be considered White, even though I have strong European and Argentinian ancestry from my father's side. I'm not Latina enough to be considered Latina, especially because I speak broken Spanish, not fluent Spanish. I'm not Black enough to be considered Black, even though my mother was African-American and her ancestors came from Cameroon, in Central Africa.

This is what's called colorism in the Black community.

And it's huge.

Because I'm light skinned, because I'm mixed or biracial—well, somehow I'm not considered Black by a lot of people.

Yet if I don't identify as Black, then I'm hating my own color, according to the critics.

You can't win.

I've never felt the need to choose my race, even though other people have asked me repeatedly, "What are you?"

They have said that I "have to belong somewhere."

That I have to fit into a nice, round peg.

I refuse to do that.

Yes, I am a woman of color. But that's not *all* of who I am.

All of my ancestry, all of my background, all of my ethnicities shape my decisions in life.

I'm incredibly proud of my background—and I always will be.

Joy Villa

I am proud of the person and the woman I am. I love all of my people of all different colors, along with all of my people of all the different ethnic backgrounds from which I'm descended.

Yet I am so much more than just the physical body I was born into, which I had no role in choosing.

This doesn't mean that I'm ashamed of anything. I'm not. I simply don't feel the need to broadcast all of my personal background at all times or to "choose" a race merely to make others feel more comfortable.

You see, people are uncomfortable with strong voices and strong individuals that they can't figure out, that they can't pigeonhole. They're uncomfortable with voices that refuse to be timid but that have a strong timbre.

People are uncomfortable with those of us who fight against preconceived notions with a smile.

We are "happy conservatives," as I heard Laura Ingraham of Fox News' *The Ingraham Angle* say from the podium at the Faith and Freedom Coalition conference a few years ago. That's an event I was and am proud to speak at myself, alongside such luminaries as President Donald J. Trump and Vice President Mike Pence, plus conservative author and filmmaker Dinesh D'Souza and so many others.

I don't use my race as an excuse in any way for anything. But I believe a lot of Black and brown people do, unfortunately.

They use their color to absolve them of responsibility. They say, "The White man's holding me down," "the White man's making me feel this way," "the White man's keeping me from having a job"—or from paying their child support, or taking care of their family, or whatever it is that's relevant to them.

I say to them: That is not true.

You and you alone are doing that to yourself.

Stop blaming others. Take responsibility.

Get to Work!

Systemic racism does exist. But it is not as all-encompassing, pervasive, or huge as the liberal media would have you believe.

Jim Crow was systemic racism. Laws that prevented interracial couples from marrying—that was systemic racism. There were whole economic systems built on slavery, not just on this continent, of course, but on others as well since time immemorial.

Today we have freedoms that our ancestors never knew.

Instead of complaining and feeling, "I still don't have enough," or, "Other people still owe me so much," we should be rejoicing and embracing, as Black people, the freedoms we have that our ancestors fought for, bled for, and suffered for—and, yes, that White people fought for, too. White people shed their blood for our freedoms, too, right alongside all the incredible Black heroes of our past.

Our nation is not perfect. But let's stop all the feelings of victimhood. We are not living on stolen land. We are living on land that was fought for and hard-won.

Many of the actions of the past may not have been moral, but our nation was built during times when people fought for the things they needed.

As a person of Native-American heritage, I mourn the loss of freedoms suffered by so many tribes during the 1800s, the sicknesses that prevailed among so many of the people, and everything else that was done to and that happened to the Native Americans. But I have a problem with those who constantly complain and say that "America is not free" when it is the freest country on Earth.

That is why millions of people fight to get into this country every year, legally and illegally. Because we are free.

Our land is a land of *freedom.*

There is no better place on Earth to be a woman, to be a person of color.

The best place to be is here, *period.*

In America, you can run for office if you choose.

You can join the police force.

You can open a business.

You can create to your heart's content.

You can work the land.

You can work your backside off.

No matter what country you came from originally, you can live the American dream here—in a place that our ancestors fought for, a place they gave their lives for, a place they were proud to call home. We can never forget all of the sacrifices they made for us and for our country.

We can never forget all of the blessings of our nation.

So when we talk about racism and prejudice in this country, the truth is that unfortunately, I have seen it most in my life from other Black Americans. As a light-skinned Black woman, I've been called all manner of names, with people assuming that I'm stuck up or full of myself merely because of the way I look and because of the color of my skin.

Black men have told me, "Oh, you must only like White guys because you won't date me." They say that based on nothing but my refusal to date them.

Or, I've been told by my own kind that I'm an *object.* A thing. A curiosity.

I've been called "a redbone," a term some people use to describe light-skinned Black women or multi-cultural women.

I hate being reduced to an "item" merely because of a skin tone that I didn't choose or have any control over whatsoever. I also hate it when women and men with darker skin are looked down upon by certain groups—almost always by groups of their own people.

Yes, there is inherent colorism, which is a form of prejudice. It's racism within the Black community. And it must end. As we move forward together in our country, we must stop blaming "the White man" for our problems and stop blaming "the system" for our problems.

Instead, we have to start fixing the problems from the inside out.

And how can we save the Black community? In my view, it's about education. It's about job training. It's about opportunity of all kinds and the ability of Black Americans to own their own businesses, to thrive, to lead their own successes. For Black families, it's about ending the abortion of Black babies—the statistics are insane on that.

All of this and much more needs to happen.

Props to You

And this is why, if you're reading this as a Black conservative or a conservative person of color, let me give props to you. It's not easy being a conservative of *any* color right now.

Liberals—those who are both White and Black—call us names of all kinds. We're seen as freaks. We can't exist within our communities simply because we are conservatives, because we love our country, because we love our traditions, because we love our president, and because we want our nation to be as strong as it can possibly be.

This is *wrong!*

Being a conservative of color is a big deal. And I'm proud of you. Proud of all of us.

And if you're thinking of becoming a conservative and are on your way to doing so, I applaud you, too.

Don't shy away from it just because it's difficult in today's environment. Yes, we must know the realities of what we face. But we should not back down from our true beliefs.

Speak to your family; speak to your friends about it. And most of all, speak to yourself.

Educate yourself, as I've said throughout this book and will keep saying. Never stop growing.

Use all of the chapters of this book to feed yourself intellectually, culturally, and creatively, as you would use food and water to nourish your body. Use my book as nourishment to restore a sense of focus and vitality within you.

I know it gets lonely out there—*but you are not alone.*

That goes for every other oppressed group.

We are not afraid.

We can stand up to whatever others throw at us.

To young people of color who are reading my book right now: *I'll always be with you.*

OK, so I may not always be young! But I'll always be Afro-Latina (and all the other parts of my ancestry as well).

And I'm here with you, now, tomorrow, and for the rest of my life.

Stand Up to Cancel Culture

Not long ago I was featured in a video about cancel culture by Jubilee Media—you can check that out on YouTube and see some of the things I say there. And guess who mentioned it?

PewDiePie. He's the world's biggest YouTuber; he's made over $20 million there. He started off as a gamer.

I absolutely love him.

I've been a fan of PewDiePie for the last three years, often bingeing on his videos, and I was delighted—I was *fangirling!*—when he took that Jubilee video and decided to offer some commentary about it. He agreed with what I said about cancel culture and called me a smart person.

Stand up to whatever others throw at you!

Among other things on that video, I said, "I have literally gotten death threats for expressing my public opinions on politics, on my support of the president." But "I'm not going to stop expressing my opinions," I added.

I also said that I don't feel safe doing it.

That's the reality of what's going on right now.

PewDiePie is in agreement with me. It was great to see and I appreciate that. (I think he might be a secret conservative!) He remains independent as a Swede living in the U.K.

I have high hopes for young people like myself, for millennials and for people in the arts. Yet it's hard when the cancel culture of today tells us that we must accept everything "they"—the liberals, the leftists, the progressives—want to shove down our throats.

Some of them even tell us that men have periods just as women do; that gender doesn't really exist; and that we should put a "cis" in front of our name if we keep the same gender throughout our lives as the one we were born with.

I love and support trans individuals, including my friend, YouTuber Blaire White; my younger brother; and many others. But I don't support the media's oversaturation of, and hyperfocus on, transgenderism today.

I don't believe in gender erasure or the notion of "gender neutral." That hurts trans existence, ironically enough.

Yet I also don't believe that you have to say and do only what your gender "tells you" that you must say and do. Sure, there are gender roles—but a person's biological sex *does exist*. It shouldn't be blurred.

Sex clearly exists. It's a fact of a person's life.

It's interesting that these people are trying to change the definition of gender today to refer only to the role a person encompasses. For example, they believe that someone could be born into a woman's body, a body of the female sex. But if that person suddenly "decides" to be male, well, OK, then that's the person's gender now and everyone else should get used to it. Absolutely ridiculous.

And as I noted in my previous chapter about femininity and feminism, just because you're born as a woman doesn't mean you can't be a truck driver. And just because you're born as a man doesn't mean you can't be a stay-at-home dad.

We all know people who do jobs that are traditionally "outside" of their gender—and I think that's the way it should be, if you so desire.

All of this is so important.

And we've got to stand up for what we believe and what we know is right.

There's a lot of nonsense out there.

We've got to call it as we see it.

NOW, HERE'S MY REAL-LIFE TIP FOR YOU if you're a conservative person of color and you're up against today's cancel culture: Stay true to your beliefs!

Remain steadfast.

Be who you are.

And don't let the "crowd" persuade you to "be" something you're not, or to say or do things you're not comfortable with, or that don't represent who you truly are or what you truly believe. Reach out to those of us who are in your shoes.

Join our groups.

Be part of the healthy conversations and interactions that we engage in as conservatives of color.

Know that you are not alone.

Stay strong!

When you check out my recommended reading list at the back of this book (both the books and the websites there), you'll see news, commentary, opinion, and engagement that will strengthen you and fortify you for the journey ahead, for this fascinating and inspiring path that we're following in 2020 and beyond.

Yep, I believe in staying positive in the face of all the negativity out there.

Sure, we have to know what's going on. But we also have to plow ahead with conviction, strength, and love.

CHAPTER 7

Homelessness, Sexual Abuse, and Suicidal Thoughts

How I Faced My Traumas to Heal—and Found My
Purpose in Life (Including My JoyTribe Mindset)

*"Come to me, all you who are weary and burdened,
and I will give you rest." —Matthew, 11:28*

I'VE SHARED A LITTLE bit about my personal life already in this book. I've been real with you throughout. Now let me share some more—*a lot more.*

My mom and dad both spoke Italian and enjoyed that way of life—it was something they shared between them. So I was raised very Italian. Food, music, Jesus, and fellowship all permeated our California household.

As a kid, I'd come home from school to the delicious smell of garlic and onions crackling in olive oil as my mom prepared dinner. My dad—Italian and Argentinian, as I've mentioned—was a pastor, and my mom—Black and Native-American—sang gospel music. The music of Kirk Franklin and Mahalia Jackson would blare from the speakers as I'd hug my laughing

A very young me, with my dad in California. I miss my parents every day.

mama and dip into my room to finish my advanced placement homework and do some drawing and painting.

Add my pursuit of art to everything I mentioned above—food, music, Jesus, and fellowship. All of it was a major part of my life growing up in California with my younger sister (who's now my transgender brother, and unfortunately doesn't speak to me), and my adopted older brother Ryjin, a brilliant performer and musician, and one of my best friends in present time, thank God.

My family was wealthy when I was in elementary school.

My Vietnam-era Army veteran dad owned his own company, raising funds for charities and hiring veterans. He traveled from Santa Barbara, California, to Manhattan regularly.

I had cats, dogs, music, and my stay-at-home mom.

Things were blissful.

Until they weren't.

Earth-Shattering Cycle

My parents' best friend and our neighbor began molesting me when I was four years old. This brutal reality left me with emotional scars that later played out in a sick and twisted opera of sexual exploits, which—many years later now—I am strong enough to affectionately call my sex, drugs, and rock 'n' roll period.

As I entered middle school, my family took a massive deep dive financially. We endured an earth-shattering cycle of hard times after that, to the point that we went from a four-bedroom, 3,500-square-foot home in beautiful suburbia with three cars to losing it *all*.

Destitute and evicted, we were now homeless.

We lived in a van in Santa Barbara County for months until my dad could find a job doing janitorial work at Walmart.

I had only music and my private prayers to get me through some nights where I was just left confused and crying.

We finally got into a motel, where I worked selling Pokémon cards and custom drawings to bring in money for our family. I hustled, I worked, I shopped at thrift stores, and I told the kids at school that we were fine. Because I had such high reading comprehension and was taught how to communicate well, they thought I was rich for living in a motel! Through all the hard times, I knew my parents loved me. That was never in doubt. They were just fallible human beings who made some very wrong choices.

And all of these years later, I miss them both terribly, unbelievably. I'm beyond thankful for their love and for giving me life.

The Search for Emotional Acceptance

I was repressed emotionally as a teenager. We finally got into an apartment, and I even had my own room. (I've always loved having my own space to create.) I drew, I painted, I sang, I wrote songs to myself, and I began modeling for some local photographers.

I felt too weird to belong, too old to be so young, and too aware overall.

I hated high school even though I excelled academically in my advanced placement classes. My relationships with my kind teachers were everything to me, and I so desperately wanted to be liked, admired, and appreciated.

I wanted to be seen.

I felt like a unicorn among buffalo. I didn't fit in.

It was also around this time that I got addicted to online porn. (Again, I'm being honest about my life.) This is something that took me years to work through. I struggled with an uncanny sexual desire after having been abused in this way at such a young age. It unleased a desire I felt shame for—yet at the same time, I felt I couldn't stop it.

After high school, there wasn't anything I didn't try or do for a while.

I was "try-sexual," and I took drugs and alcohol to further numb the trauma that tried to resurface from my earlier years. I went from man to man, woman to woman, looking for emotional acceptance and rest from the pain in another's embrace.

It felt so good to drink, get high, find a sexy stranger, and let go for a moment, feeling finally accepted and "normal." But then I'd wake up, sober and alone again, with depressive thoughts and a suffocating sense of loneliness.

Again, I am sharing this with all of you so that you know how far I've come from the hard times I've experienced. And if you're going through hard times yourself right now, I want you to know that you can, and you will, come out of them.

There is a light at the end of the tunnel. *As there was for me!*

For a while, nothing seemed to help me back then, not the constant parties or the blur of faces occupying my bedroom, not the pot, the pills, or the exotic clothes that were part of my life at that time.

I sang lead in a metal band (which quickly fell apart). I did some more modeling and was part of some burlesque dance troupes. My artistic and creative instincts drew me to some of this activity, but things became darker in nature as time went on.

And it was during this period of my life that I wrote my hit song "The Darkness," which is on my No. 1 Billboard rock album, "I Make The Static." You'll see exactly how I felt at that time and where I was in my thinking when you read the full lyrics to "The Darkness," which I'm including here for you to see.

What I wrote then is *very* revealing.

"THE DARKNESS"
by Joy Villa

I'll walk away
Pretending everything's okay
It burns the pavement of my soul

I know the truth
What I did before did me no good
These scars prove my pain

'Cause I don't wanna live in the darkness
I wanna step into the light
'Cause I can't stay in the darkness
It's seepin' into my soul
It's seepin' into my soul
And it's all that I've known
It's all that I've known

I'll turn the page
A new story, a new face
I made the change for myself

A heart to heart
Love has passed and now I feel alone
This quill writes the song

'Cause I don't wanna live in the darkness
I wanna step into the light
'Cause I can't stay in the darkness
It's seepin' into my soul
It's seepin' into my soul
And it's all that I've known
It's all that I've known

This hole has no place
Suffering needs change
And I am breathing like it's the first time
Sunshine dries rain
Spirit needs space
And I am seeing like it's the first time
This hole has no place
Suffering needs change
I am breathing like it's the first time
Sunshine dries rain
Spirit needs space
I am seeing like it's the first time

'Cause I don't wanna live in the darkness
I wanna step into the light
'Cause I can't stay in the darkness
It's seepin' into my soul
It's seepin' into my soul
And it's all that I've known
It's all that I've known

'Cause I don't wanna live in the darkness
I wanna step into the light
'Cause I can't stay in the darkness
It's seepin' into my soul
It's seepin' into my soul
And it's all that I've known
It's all that I've known

By now I had lost my mom, survived an abusive relationship, and given up my very own precious baby for adoption—all within the same year.

And that's when I was just 20 years old.

My past of sexual abuse came rushing up at me and I wanted to feel powerful and in control—instead of oh-so-weak and vulnerable. As a result, I put myself in dangerous, harmful situations, thinking of my body as a worthless tool to use and abuse. I formed a dependency on alcohol, pot, and sex.

I am strong enough now to admit this and put it out like this.

And in my darkest months, I even started working in a strip club.

Wearying of that and then *further* depressed, I joined an agency as an upscale escort, selling my body to pay bills and numb my aching soul. But I still didn't feel worthy of real love or any real connections. I went through relationships like water, dating weak men to feel powerful.

I finally circled *soooo* down the drain that I couldn't pay my rent on my Hollywood apartment.

Dishes piled up in the kitchen sink and roaches roamed the cold bathroom tiles at night. I spent any money I made on drinks, drugs, and shiny clothes, wanting desperately to feel normal and pretty.

Finally, I was evicted. I became homeless.

At that point I started couch-jumping to survive. I even abused the kindness of my older brother until his roommates kicked me out.

Yet again, I was scared and alone, too proud to ask my poor dad for help, even though deep down I knew he loved me.

I was utterly ashamed.

Every night I cried out to God in agony. I pleaded with Him to help me.

I even thought of taking my own life at one point, as I already felt it had been destroyed and deemed worthless. And I had horrible thoughts in my head of what that would look like.

I can't believe how different my life is today, looking back. I can't believe what I went through.

How did such a bright and brilliant "good girl" end up used, abused, and washed up—and depending on the kindness of strangers in a cold city like Hollywood? How did I make it out to the other side?

God pulled me through.

Again, if any of you are in a rough spot or a troubled time, I'm here to tell you: You can fight your way out! You will make it!

You are worth it. ALWAYS.

As I was and as *I am today. ALWAYS.*

Also, service can be a wonderful thing. Let me explain.

Agony—and Redemption

After alcohol and sex addictions overtook my life and I sank to my darkest of times, I cried out to God, asking Him, "Where are the others like me? How can I be used to help them? What is my purpose?"

God illuminated that for me. He showed me again that my purpose is to be a beacon for those who need help. But to do that, I had to help myself first.

I finally let go of everything—the pride, the ego, the anger at my parents for letting bad things happen to me, the anger at myself for not living up to my potential, for giving up my dreams, for giving up my own precious daughter for adoption even though I knew then (and still know now) that it was the best decision for both of us. Yet it still cut me to my core. I thought I didn't deserve to have children because of my reckless behavior, my drinking, my partying ways, my sexual depravity at that time.

Somehow, I also felt that I didn't deserve love, that I could never be a wife or a mother or have a successful career, or be someone who helped millions of others by sharing her goodness, her truth as a warrior, and her voice. I felt as if I didn't *have* any voice at all.

But God reached down and reminded me that my voice *is* valuable. He reminded me that my actions had not lived up to the standards I had set for myself (or that He had set for me!). He reminded me of things that I'd forgotten.

I reached out to a friend to drive me to the hospital. And I fully committed my life back to God as I spent weeks in the hospital recovering from the damage I had done to myself, to my body, my mind, and my soul—the lack of sleep, the drinking, the pot, the poor nutrition, the stress, everything.

From the hospital I was admitted to a rehab program for 30 days. And that's when I truly began to see my way out—to know that I would make it, with God's help.

A girl who bunked next to me had a book that she was reading, and I said, "What's that?"

She showed it to me. She said, "I'm in AA."

And I said, "Oh, that could help me."

She described the "Serenity Prayer" to me, the essence of which is,

"God, grant me the serenity to accept the things I cannot change, the courage to change the things I can, and the wisdom to know the difference." (I include some resources on AA and other organizations in my reading list at the back of the book.) And when she described how this friendly prayer had helped her heal, immediately a light bulb went off in my head.

I thought: *Maybe I'm not insane, as my mom had been.* The doctors had forced my mom to take drugs for years to help her (supposedly), but they didn't. Instead, those drugs damaged her liver and tranquilized her into a zombie. I knew I didn't want to throw drugs down my throat like that. (This is why I believe that the big pharma companies and the psychiatric drugging of people are *wrong.*) And while I now understood that I had an alcohol addiction problem, I also knew that I had not properly recovered from the traumas I'd suffered earlier in my life.

I started healing. I started attending Alcoholics Anonymous meetings. And I stayed clean and sober through acts of service, daily prayer, and my music. I attended regular AA meetings, went to church three times a week, and began developing a new community for myself through my volunteer work, including at a church. I played my guitar every night and began writing songs again, no longer numbed by alcohol, pot, and partying.

I was staying with my dad after I finished rehab, and he and I began restoring our relationship. We healed as father and daughter. We worked through *everything.* And he affirmed me, acknowledging that I did not have to take pills if I didn't want to (a doctor had prescribed them to me at one point).

And I remember very consciously realizing, through all of my healing during this period, that I was finding my sense of purpose again and becoming, again, the beautiful daughter of Christ that I had always been.

I knew that I had suffered from depression and anxiety, but also from trauma. The answer wasn't to blame others or to be beholden forever to anyone, including the government.

And this is not to put down people who truly do suffer from mental disturbances and truly need help. I just knew (and still know) that exercise, prayer, music, meditation, and acts of service to others all worked for me.

Everything reignited now. I was playing music and journaling every day. I started painting and drawing again. I found my voice again. Today (as I've also noted elsewhere in this book), I regularly receive spiritual counseling, attend church, and have a strong community that I serve.

Even though I'm not a preacher, as my dad was, I can follow in his footsteps to an extent as a preacher's kid. I'm flawed, but I use my vulnerability to help others.

And this is what being a strong, independent, conservative woman is all about for me! I want to help others understand the dangers of socialism, the false promises of feminism, and the recklessness and errors of a YOLO ("you only live once") attitude. I believe that life is precious. I believe that we are eternal beings and that what we do today impacts tomorrow. We must take care of ourselves emotionally, mentally, spiritually, and physically so that we can fight the good fight for justice, for free speech, and for American values.

I hope that my story will help you, my readers, no matter where you are in your own journey as a conservative and as a human, to fully grab your future.

You can change the outcome of your own life. If you're not happy with an aspect of your life, make a change. Do something about it.

It's not easy, but I fight every day to work through my issues, to be a strong woman, and to become (I hope!) a strong mother again and a strong wife again.

Pushing Forward

If you happen to be depressed or down or stuck at this moment in time, it might be because you've stopped going after what makes you happy and started pleasing everyone else. That's partly what happened to me.

My advice is: Fill your own cup first. *Then* you'll be ready to serve others.

And let the guilt go. Guilt only keeps people broken and inept. Let's stop staying in victimhood and start living victoriously.

F*** guilt! F*** shame!

(Why is it OK for people to self-insult but not self-compliment? We need to love ourselves and say often how powerful and amazing we are. *You're amazing! I'm amazing!*)

Art of all kinds kept me sane then and continues to heal me today. I'm proud to be both an artist and an introvert, even though being sensitive at times is very rough. I feel things deeply, yet I have no choice but to create out of that.

I now began acting in some small films and other roles (there's much more about my start in the entertainment business in the next chapter, too). I had done some modeling earlier, so I continued doing some of that. And I was volunteering at a church in Sherman Oaks when I met a friend of a friend, a producer named Mr. Skip-A-Beat. He and I began working together and creating music. He said to me, "When I see you, I hear music."

We started working on what would become my first-ever professionally produced song, "Cold Wind," which I wrote in 10 minutes.

That's usually what happens when I write my best music. It comes pouring out of me. It's the muse blessing me with her silky touch!

The song is really about my spiritual journey, which continues to this day.

Check out the lyrics that follow.

"COLD WIND"
by Joy Villa

Ahhh Ahhh
I was lost
Lost in the sand
Just a grain
I didn't know where to stand

Enter you
Vibrant right where you were
And I never predicted
That this would occur

'Cause you came around me
Like a cold wind
A cold wind
Yeah you did
You came around me
Like a cold wind,
A cold wind
Yeah you did

Ahhhhh
My breath
Seemed to be passing me by
So many lifetimes spent
Just searching for the light
I didn't expect any new thing
But you set the game
And now I'm ready to win

'Cause you came around me
Like a cold wind
A cold wind
Yeah you did
You came around me
Like a cold wind
A cold wind
Yeah you did

Ahhhhh I just felt it
The moment we melted
You came alive just the same
Like a candle we light up
It's sweet and it's bitter
We came alive in this flame
Yeah!

'Cause you came around me
Like a cold wind
A cold wind
Yeah you did
You came around me
Like a cold wind,
A cold wind
Yeah you did
Yeah, yeah

I played acoustic guitar on that song and we produced it on a shoe-string budget. From there, Mr. Skip-A-Beat introduced me to ASCAP (the American Society of Artists and Performers), which I joined, and I went on to meet other musicians and artists.

That year of 2011, everything broke out for me.

I started playing gigs with my guitar. I knew that music was my passion—not necessarily being in a band, where there can be so much drama (which I'd already experienced), but having my own band.

Today, I hire extremely capable musicians who work with me, and it works out really well!

How I Created My Healthy JoyTribe Mindset

Now, as a successful entertainer, artist, writer, and speaker, people often ask me, "How do you stay healthy and sane in a crazy world?"

After everything I've been through and as far as I've come in this life, I'm happy to share some meaningful tips with you.

I had to learn a lot of things the really, really hard way.

But learn I did.

You might want to get out a notebook at this point (if you haven't already!), as I think you will find all of this incredibly useful in your own life as you read what I'm saying here and absorb it.

You'll learn not just how to be a kickass conservative—you'll become a pretty kickass human being as well!

#1: I AM VERY SELECTIVE ABOUT THE PEOPLE I KEEP AROUND ME. Before I became a celebrity, and before I came out as a true conservative, I had a ton of "friends." They were just associates, really.

But at the time, I was calling a lot of these people my friends.

Many of them would hang around me like flies on honey, like flies on molasses. And they would drink up my honey and take from me, stealing my energy and leaving me feeling drained, exhausted, and deflated.

I learned that I had to be selective about the company I kept.

I had to stay true to myself and do what was right for me.

Unfortunately, it meant that I had to distance myself from a lot of people I really liked.

They were poison for me.

I'll be straight-up honest with you: There are plenty of shiny, glimmering, beautiful things in this world that look good but are deadly to the touch. Every rose has its thorns. No one's perfect. But the trick is to find a rose that blooms brighter than its thorns—and that's what I myself hope to be for other people.

I'm not a perfect person. And I have never claimed to be. I thank God for His grace and His mercy and for the incredible people I do have around me now. They've changed my life for the better.

Even some of the negative people I encountered over the years shared important lessons with me, whether they knew it or not.

But I'll tell you this: Even salt looks like sugar at times.

Be very aware and careful of those you let into your inner circle. Be fair, but use discernment.

Be wise in your judgment toward individuals who claim they want to help you. Their "help" may actually be a knife in the back.

Et tu, Brute? Remember that line from the play "Julius Caesar" by William Shakespeare? It's what Caesar said as he was being murdered by his own friend, Brutus, who was among all the other assassins.

So, yes: "Even you, Brutus?"

Today, I don't put up with nonsense from people, and I actively vet those I work with. I also won't work with someone who wants to do something for free for me. I believe in paying people what they're worth.

These are good policies to set up early on in any business endeavors.

As an entrepreneur, it's important for me to have clear policies and to know what I want at all times.

Think about that for yourself if you're planning on starting a business.

#2: *I DON'T DO DRUGS, I DON'T DRINK ALCOHOL, AND I DON'T SMOKE.* Having had horrible experiences with drinking and drugs, as I mentioned earlier, I know how harmful these addictions can be.

In the initial stages, when you take those things, they seem to solve everything. They can calm you down, help you relax, help you chill out. But in the end, all you're doing is pushing away the issues you need to confront. After you sober up, the problems are still there, glaring at you, staring you in the face—still needing to be addressed.

So I keep a very clean body. I don't do any drugs. I don't smoke cigarettes. Those things are all terrible for you and will not enrich your life in any way.

I'm forever grateful to God that He saved me from so much degradation.

Today, I drink a gallon of water or more every day. I also get plenty of sleep—eight or nine hours a night. Plus, I take a whole-food multivitamin. (I really like the vitamin company Thorne, by the way, as they don't use any fillers. It's all plant-based. It's the one my doctor prescribes for me; it's for those with sensitivities and intolerance, and is made without artificial ingredients.)

And back to drugs and alcohol for a moment: The National Institute on Drug Abuse (NIDA) has reported that by the time young people reach their senior year of high school, 70 percent of kids will have tried alcohol, 50 percent will have abused an illicit drug, 40 percent will have smoked a cigarette, and 20 percent will have used a prescription drug—either recreationally or for nonmedical purposes.

Alcohol is the number-one substance of abuse for this young demographic. And marijuana is the top drug of choice, according to the U.S. Department of Health and Human Services (HHS) Office of Adolescent Health.

Bottom line is that many people under age 30 are on some sort of drug, which is an outrage to me.

These young people—and you may be one of them—*are the future of our country!*

Drugs and alcohol numb you. Well, guess what? I don't want to be numb. I want to be alive. Don't you?

I want to be fully aware—spiritually aware, too—and able to perceive and feel everything I can. Don't you?

Drugs, including pharmaceuticals, have done more harm than good in our society. I don't want any part of that. I have come through to the other side: I am staunchly anti-drug and that includes all drugs—pot, pills, you name it.

Also, I love coffee. But caffeine is a drug as well. I realized I had to give up what I was doing in order to be my healthiest. So I went from drinking four cups of black coffee a day—plus maybe a latte—to two cups of green tea a day.

Yeah, I went from drinking caffeine a *latte* to just a little (I know, *groooooan!*).

Every once in a while, I'll have a coffee because I'm a coffee snob and I just love the comforting taste of it. But it's rare for me now.

And because of the way I've taken care of myself for years, I have flourished and prospered.

I know this is no accident.

I want this for all of you, too.

#3: I EAT HEALTHY, WHOLE FOODS. I GET LOTS OF EXERCISE.

I've been a vegan for 16 years. I eat a healthy, whole-food, vegan diet. I eat whole vegetables—organic whenever possible—and I try to eat as much as 50 percent raw foods.

Being vegan keeps my physique sleek and my body-fat percentage low, as well as giving my skin a healthy glow.

Eating this way has been amazing for me. I went vegan at age 18, and it completely cleared my acne, which I used to suffer from as a teenager. No more! I'm a vegan for ethical reasons. I adore animal lives and wouldn't think of consuming them for food. Veganism is sustainable for the earth.

I work hard for the body I have! Keeping myself physically fit is key to a healthy, happy life.

And in terms of good health, I want to live longer and be able to be there for my future children and grandchildren.

I also exercise an hour a day, five days a week. I jog, I run stairs, I lift heavy weights—and oh, yes, I do my squats and deadlifts!

In 2016, I entered my first competition for bikini bodybuilding held by the National Physique Committee. I earned a gorgeous third-place trophy.

I placed fourth in my weight class and third in the open class, which is a lot harder. I trained my body and mind in extreme physical fitness, working out several hours a day for four months to whip my body into shape. Stage competition is tough! It's given me a lot of discipline and I use it in politics and life today.

At my height of 5'10" and 165-175 pounds, I was a lean, green, fighting machine—and fully plant-based. Love it!

I continue to bodybuild today and I look forward to my next competition in bikini bodybuilding. (I'd even like to go pro.) This is all part of my discipline and my integrity to my body and to physical fitness.

You don't have to enter competitions as I did, but you can dedicate yourself to some form of physical fitness, whether it's walking, gardening, running, or dancing. (I've also danced professionally—danced for years! I grew up dancing as a girl. I did gymnastics and ran track in high school, winning medals for track as a high school athlete. I've been athletic my whole life.)

Ladies, don't be afraid to pick up the weights. A lot of you already do, which is great. We need to lift weights for our muscle tone and to keep our bodies fit.

Whatever you do to stay physically fit, even just 30 minutes a day of exercise can change your outlook. Physical fitness has been proven to be more effective in treating depression than antidepressant medication.

As an introvert, I find that my "alone time" with my headphones on in the gym or while pounding a punching bag in my apartment can be a beautiful and cathartic experience. It's one that I lovingly call #self-care.

It is really important to our well-being!

#4: I BELIEVE IN THE POWER OF POSITIVE THINKING, THE POWER OF PRAYER, AND THE POWER OF LEARNING. I'm a believer in staying positive. I believe in prayer and in spirituality. I go to church regularly, and I lay down my burdens in prayer to God.

I was raised in a strict Christian household. Today, I have my own sense of spirituality, of what God is to me, of who God is to me. My Christian faith is very important to me. And I've sought out spiritual counseling over the years to help me understand, process, and heal from my past traumas.

Having been through my journey of surrendering to God, of giving my life back over to Him, I know that all of us can recover from our struggles. Everyone can recover from substance abuse, from self-harm, from shame, from guilt, from anything that takes us away from being the incredible beings we were created to be. I captured these sentiments in my song "Surrender."

"SURRENDER"
by Joy Villa

There's so much life I've left to live
And this fire is burning still
When I watch you look at me

I think I could find the will
To stand for every dream
And forsake this solid ground
And give up this fear within
Of what would happen if they ever knew
I'm in love with you

'Cause I'd surrender everything
To feel the chance to live again
I reach to you
I know you can feel it too
We'd make it through
A thousand dreams I still believe
I'd make you give them all to me
I'd hold you in my arms and never let go
I surrender

I know I can't survive
Another night away from you
You're the reason I go on
And now I need to live the truth

Right now, there's no better time
From this fear I will break free
And I'll live again with love
And no they can't take that away from me
And they will see ...

I'd surrender everything
To feel the chance to live again
I reach to you
I know you can feel it too
We'd make it through
A thousand dreams I still believe
I'd make you give them all to me
I'd hold you in my arms and never let go
I surrender

Every night's getting longer
And this fire is getting stronger, baby
I'll swallow my pride and I'll be alive
Can't you hear my call
I surrender all

I'd surrender everything
To feel the chance to live again
I reach to you
I know you can feel it too
We'll make it through
A thousand dreams I still believe
I'll make you give them all to me
I'll hold you in my arms and never let go
I surrender

Right here, right now
I give my life to live again
I'll break free, take me
My everything, I surrender all to you

Right now
I give my life to live again
I'll break free, take me
My everything, I surrender all to you

Also, there are a few books that have helped me in my life and that continue to help me today. I'll mention some here; they are by no means the only ones.

The book *Dianetics*, a best-selling book on mental health by L. Ron Hubbard (who founded Scientology), has helped me a great deal, along with the course that goes with it. It helped me wade through a lot of mental garbage in my life that came up from the past. It has worked wonders for me, and it will help you, too.

(Be sure to check out my suggested reading list at the back of this book.)

The 5 Love Languages by Gary Chapman has also aided me tremendously in my relationships, in knowing what "love language" to use with various people, and to communicate better and operate at a higher level. Take the test and learn for yourself!

Also, *Men Are from Mars, Women Are from Venus* by John Gray, Ph.D., has helped me sort out various scenarios in my dating life. It explains the difference between masculine and feminine energy. It's a great read, an oldie but goodie.

Something else that I read a lot, and have read many, many times, is the Book of Proverbs in the Holy Bible. I have read and studied this amazing book of wisdom since I was a child.

The Book of Proverbs is a favorite. Many classic sayings have come from this book—people forget that—and it's brought me great comfort

Staying positive in the face of negativity is really important to me.

over the years and set me up on a good path to value the right things.

I enjoy reading as many books as I can.

I enjoy listening to audiobooks.

And my advice for others is this: Study. Learn. Improve yourself.

Add to your knowledge base regularly.

Take courses and classes.

It's not just about being a kickass conservative.

It's about being a kickass individual!

#5: I PRACTICE GRATITUDE EVERY DAY. IT'S A KEY PART OF MY #SELF-CARE. I keep a gratitude journal. I write things down that I'm grateful for; I jot down my thoughts and feelings.

I also take long walks in nature whenever I can. I get sunshine on my skin and feel the fresh air.

I spend time with loved ones. I get and give lots of hugs and kisses, lots of affection. And if you're in a committed relationship, as I am, lots of sex is a smart idea, too!

All of these things contribute to good health.

I think healthy thoughts. I take baths, light candles, and listen to music, especially during stressful times. #Self-care is extremely important. Being out there in the world, as a conservative as I am, can be very stressful. I have to know what's going on, so I'm always paying attention to the news of the day.

Perhaps you're in the same boat!

And I'm a target, as I've mentioned earlier—so I have to take care of myself to stay healthy through all of this.

I surround myself with loved ones and with good relationships that help me thrive and stay strong, and feel powerful and beautiful.

My girlfriends have been there for me through thick and thin, too.

I have beautiful girlfriends. And I'm grateful for each and every one of them. They're also incredible conservatives who have supported me since the very beginning.

Yes, there are a lot of snakes in the grass out there, as I've mentioned once or twice in this book by now. But there are also beautiful fellow lions and tigers—*lionesses* and *tigresses!*—who will walk with you through the pain and stand by your side.

And I can't forget the power of having goals and purposes in life. Write those down. Reflect on them. Focus on them.

We don't get anywhere meaningful in our lives without purposefully, consciously aiming for what we want.

With the help of a site called www.wise.org and a tool called the Admin Scale, I've been able to articulate my purpose, goals, and desires—and plan exactly how to turn those into something actual. ("Wise" in that URL stands for World Institute of Scientology Enterprises, but it's used by businesses and individuals from all walks of life.)

I know what I want and how to get it. I've found a clean, easy, and simple way to work toward success and achieve the things I care about.

It works for me.

NOW, HERE'S MY REAL-LIFE TIP FOR YOU to improve your life and achieve the things you want now and in the years ahead: I've outlined a lot of steps in this chapter and shared with you the things I do that work for me.

I came out of some very hard times, as I noted—and I am grateful beyond measure for all that I have achieved so far, with God's help.

There's so much more to come!

Each of us needs to dig deep to think about our lives, what we want most, and what matters to us. We can't allow ourselves to be "carried" along or directed by others. That is the path to disappointment and even danger.

You may need to spend some quiet time on your own, thinking deeply and without interruption, and writing down what you want to achieve in life.

I can guarantee you that God wants you to succeed in your path. He's given you and each of us an amazing array of abilities and talents.

We need to use them!

There are no excuses on this planet that can stop you from your divine future, from your divine path. This is an integral part of how I live my life and my philosophy, and that's why this book is not just about my conservative journey—but my own *personal* journey.

And I want you to know—everyone who's reading this book with me—that you, too, can achieve greatness. You, too, can dominate your sector, your sphere of influence. You, too, can rise and expand like a pebble dropped into a lake.

Like ripples in the water, your influence can expand—but it's up to you to make the first step, the first move.

Never give up on yourself.

Believe in yourself, now more than ever.

Work to make yourself healthier. Take care of yourself. Value yourself.

And be the best version of yourself that you can be.

There is no one else like you, *period*.

CHAPTER 8

Freedom: Fight for It!

My Beliefs Shape My Character and Vision

"More freedom, not more government, is the answer."
—Republican Gov. Kristi Noem of South Dakota

WHEN I VOTED FOR Trump four years ago, in November 2016, I felt I had to be closeted about it. Just sayin' it here (and in a few other places), so that you're knowin' it!

I thought I had to be quiet about my true beliefs when I voted for the Republican—and not the Democrat—for president of the United States.

Many other people, including a lot of my friends, felt that way, too.

And many others likely do even now.

We felt we would face backlash forever if we let our friends, colleagues, neighbors, and even members of our own families know what we truly believed and how we really voted, as I said on Fox News not that long ago and to others as well, including Jesse Lee Peterson.

But once Trump was elected in a stunning victory for our country, and as the new year of 2017 began, I decided, for my part, that I was through with holding it all in.

My journey to conservatism had been an internal process, as things like this often are—and now it was time to use my voice about it.

I had to be myself. I had to let people know how I felt, let them know that I'd grown into my conservatism over a period of time and was finally ready to announce it.

And I decided I wanted to be—that I *had* to be—an activist for the things I hold dear.

My deepest beliefs are about love and unifying for the country, and about unifying around this president.

It was time for me to let the world know that.

Let Freedom Ring

I believe in freedom. I believe in America, in our First Amendment and Second Amendment rights, in our ability to control our own lives and our own destinies, and in all the traditions that our great country has stood for—many of which are under powerful attack right now and have been for years.

I believe in putting America first.

I believe in a strong America.

I believe in the individual and in the individual's rights.

I believe in conservative values—which include respect for American traditions, Republicanism, support for Christian values, individualism, and a defense of Western culture "from the perceived threats posed by socialism, authoritarianism, and moral relativism," as Wikipedia notes, in part.

And, as that site also notes (and please see my list of recommended reading list for conservatives at the back of this book), "As with all major American political parties, liberty is a core value. American conservatives consider individual liberty—within the bounds of America—as the fundamental trait of democracy; this perspective contrasts with that of modern

Be patriotic for America and for all that's good in our nation!

American liberals, who generally place a greater value on equality and social justice, and emphasize the need for state intervention to achieve these goals."

This is why I feel it is absolutely critical that we reelect President Donald J. Trump in November 2020 so that the United States of America can remain as strong, free, safe, and secure as possible.

I say all of this as a proud and free American.

I say it with conviction and confidence as an outspoken musician, artist, and activist who happens to be based in Hollywood.

And let me tell you something: Hollywood's a really tough place to be a conservative.

With this empowering personal statement of mine (and others throughout this book), I hope you'll feel motivated as you take your own journey in life as a conservative who wants to save our country.

I am a creator and an artist. No one controls me. No one tells me what to do or what not to do when it comes to my music, my lyrics, my art, and any of my creative activities—no matter where I work or what kind of work I do.

That's a beautiful and important thing.

And it's worth fighting for, privately and publicly.

I speak my mind, and I speak up. I create my music and my art on a daily basis, and I share my messages in an authentic, personal, and meaningful way.

It's the *only* way I can imagine going through this amazing life of ours.

To think that I dreamed of doing all of this and more as a kid—and now I'm living out those dreams and making them happen. *Incredible.*

And if someone, by the way, is going to judge me by the color of my skin and the texture of my hair, I say strongly to that person: Love me for my values, not for the way I look.

All of this is why I released my single, "Freedom (Fight for It)," last summer. (Go to www.joyvilla.com for that song and more.) It's just as relevant today, in this year of 2020, with a presidential election ahead of us.

Freedom definitely isn't free. We have to go to battle in many ways to preserve our freedom.

And it's about fighting the hate—fighting the censorship that exists in our society and *especially* in liberal circles today.

In my song, I refer to the "mental prison," the "slavery of the mind" that exists too often today on the left.

"Propaganda controls our youth," I sing.

"Stone culture—broken truth."

And in the chorus, I sing: "Freedom! Do you really want to live free? Do you really want to be free? You gotta fight for it! You better fight for it!"

Didn't Come by This Lightly

As I've told many of you before, I'd been a full-on feminist and left-leaning independent who lived in New York City after I moved there from the West Coast—and now I was back on the West Coast, working in Hollywood.

I'd voted (twice!) for our first Black president, Barack Obama, and I traveled the world, proud to be non-political unless it involved social justice warriors.

Oh, I was a #SJW to the hilt! I even pushed the candidacy of Bernie Sanders there for a period of time, as I mentioned earlier in this book.

And then, to the shock and horror of so many people, I came out as a bonafide, pro-life, pro-God, pro-freedom, pro-America Trumplican in February 2017.

What was going on?

As you've been finding out in these pages, it wasn't an overnight decision. Not at all.

But I knocked the socks off people because they had no idea it was coming. By stunning so many Americans with my true and passionate beliefs, I began to attract my fair share of haters, as I referenced a bit earlier—and yeah, the ugly death threats began to pour into my social media and email inboxes.

And even my best friend since middle school disowned me for being a Trump supporter as an Afro-Latina woman. This person—a gay Black man—couldn't fathom staying friends with me, even though nothing had changed about me or our friendship, except that I'd now expressed public support for a president I knew had the guts to fight for us, the American people, rather than the special interest groups in Washington or the sick and twisted swamp that both the left and right had worshipped for decades.

And for the first time in 40 years, the Clinton Dynasty had ended.

Incredible.

Hillary's reign was finally over.

All of her dirty dealings with the special interest groups, including the pharmaceutical companies, would be behind us now.

The woman who insulted half of America in 2016 by smugly, rudely, and horribly calling us "a basket of deplorables" in front of a crowd and thinking it was fine to do that was *done*. (As I noted earlier, we won't forget that any time soon!)

For the first time in decades, there were no more Clintons in any elected office in America. *Hallelujah.*

Why do I speak out for Trump to this day, you ask?

Why do I speak out for America, for freedom, for conservative values, for our future?

Bold, True Leader

Trump's been fighting for all of us—every single one of us—throughout his presidency, including this year as we've been facing the coronavirus crisis and the stunning economic fallout from it.

He's been fighting to protect our country, fighting for each and every one of us as Americans as we go about our lives, to live as free individuals, and to do so safely and proudly.

Don't listen to the liberals when they rudely, wrongly, call Trump "racist" for referring to the coronavirus as the "Wuhan virus" or the "Chinese plague," by the way. Those are straightforward and factual statements on Trump's part.

That's where the illness originated.

But the left won't even grant him that.

Nope. They rip him to shreds for that and so much more.

They don't like someone who strongly challenges and threatens their big-government policies and agenda, and their runaway globalism.

They don't like someone who doesn't sing their tune—every single word of it.

The left doesn't want to give this president an inch. They won't even acknowledge that by closing our country's borders early on this year to travelers from China (at the end of January) and then from Europe (shortly after that), Trump thwarted the spread of the virus and prevented the possible deaths of thousands and thousands—millions, probably—of Americans.

While it is horrible that over 148,000 people (as my book goes to press) have died in the U.S. from this vicious, invisible scourge, Trump took decisive early action to close our borders and prevent what clearly would have been far more human devastation.

He also worked tirelessly on so many other fronts.

In March, he had the Navy hospital ship USNS Comfort sent to New York Harbor in response to the virus outbreak—and ditto for the USNS Mercy, which was deployed from its home base of San Diego to the L.A. area.

(USNS Comfort treated just 182 patients over nearly a month of its deployment there, ultimately returning to its base in Norfolk, Virginia. As for the USNS Mercy, it treated 77 patients during its roughly seven-week stay in the L.A. area. It, too, then returned to its home base.)

The liberal politicians in both New York and California didn't appreciate all that the president did for them. They rejected most, if not all, of his help.

Trump convened the White House Coronavirus Task Force—and

took scores of other actions that have been well documented by conservative sites and publications (but not by those on the left).

Where is the credit for Trump's strong, decisive action as a leader? For everything he did, day after day—for everything he *does*, day after day—on behalf of this country?

Not on the liberal-leaning cable outlets, that's for sure!

Of course every single life matters.

Of course every single life is precious.

I mourn for all those we've lost to the virus, and I grieve for them and their families. I know that the vast majority of those who died were older or were immunocompromised—again, it's incredibly sad and heartbreaking.

But I worry that the numbers of those infected have been inflated.

There has been so much from the World Health Organization (WHO) and so many other health "experts" that we couldn't, and still can't, trust. (For example: "Don't wear a mask. It won't help." But then—"Oh, now you must wear a mask in public, except when you're exercising!" OR: "Beware of surfaces where the virus might spread." But then—"Oh, don't worry so much about the surfaces after all." OR: "People who are asymptomatic are not going to spread the virus." But then—"Oh, never mind that advice. They might spread it after all.")

It's been dizzying, to say the least.

Also, for all of us who are young, healthy, and eager to work, did we— *do we*—really need to stay in lockdown mode for so long?

I understood the quarantining early on. I got that.

But when you put people in cages and leave them there—taking away their ability to work, their freedom to worship, their ability to keep themselves healthy by going to the gym or walking in the park or going to the beach, their ability to be with other people—well, eventually they're going to act like animals.

It's ridiculous. It's insane.

We were and have been closed for *way, way too long.*

But we will beat this virus in the end.

If any country can do it, America can.

I have confidence in our country and in President Donald J. Trump.

Bottom Line

I love our country and our president, our traditions, our values. As an American, I believe in protecting life from womb to tomb.

I am proudly pro-life.

I believe in embracing diversity while not alienating nationalistic pride.

I believe in open arms and secure borders, in strong values and happy warriors.

I support the First Amendment.

I support the Second Amendment.

I support freedom-minded and educated voters.

And I believe that we as a people must preserve our right to religious and personal freedom to express, worship, and practice our spiritual beliefs and our expression of God without government control.

There is no better person to tell someone how to live his or her life than that person himself/herself. That's something Trump knows well and completely embraces.

I want the strongest possible America for all of us and our children and grandchildren. We have a lot of hard work to do, this year and beyond.

It's why it's so important we speak out and act on behalf of our country.

I want all of us to continue to live proudly and free, in an America whose independence we jubilantly celebrate every Fourth of July, no matter what the radical liberals say. The acts of our Founding Fathers and Mothers more than 244 years ago to establish liberty from foreign and tyrannical rule can, and should, embolden us to live and embody the American dream while allowing others to do the same—minus an oppressive, overbearing socialist government.

I've been saying these things and more across this nation now for about four years—and to so many of you in my beautiful JoyTribe on various social media platforms.

Our vital conservative values are under attack simply because millions of us want life, liberty, and the pursuit of happiness.

But we are standing up for these values.

And I'm saying to all of you now: Watch out this November, when Trump is reelected.

Which he must be, to preserve our country.

And I firmly believe, in my heart and in my soul, that he *will* be.

Talkin' Trump

I'm a registered Republican today. And it's the Trumplican part of this that I care the most about.

I like this kind of Republican. I like seeing all the different colors across our country—all ages, races, religions, sexualities, and thought processes.

And I like that those of us on this side of the aisle work hard not to judge one another based on any one of those things.

We're going to look at each other, consider each other, be thoughtful, and respect each other—*unless somebody gives us a reason not to do so.*

That is the human race.

That is the American way.

Meanwhile, many liberals on the left keep talking about us—oh, and they do far more than talk.

They *rip* into our president day and night.

Yep, the late-night crowd jabbers on about almost nothing else.

They talk about what our president is tweeting, saying, doing practically every minute of the day. They mock what he looks like, who he looked *at*, the way he walks, the way he talks, and everything in between.

They spend countless hours attacking him and trying to look for new ways to do it.

(Imagine living like that, with so much hate?)

They talk about his policies and his actions for America—and almost all of what they say about our president is negative, divisive, and hysterical.

They constantly put him down as a way of trying to lift themselves up.

It's terrible. It's really, really sad.

Our president may be the hardest working and most pro-American president we have *ever* had, certainly in our lifetimes. Even if they don't like him personally, does anyone on the left ever *give* President Trump any credit for all of the good he has done for our country in his first four years in office?

For strengthening our country?

For putting America first in his words and in his actions?

Do you ever hear that on television, in any of the news sources or articles you see circulating on social media?

Rarely, if ever—let's be honest.

As we all know, the liberals, no matter who they are or where they are, too often say what they think their audience and their base want to hear— and they dish out a steady diet of negativity. It's clear that they want "their own people" in political power no matter who those people are—even Joe Biden, someone totally unfit for the highest office in the land. (More of my thoughts on Biden appear in the next chapter.)

And since they all read from the same liberal playbook, it's no wonder that some of their lines sound the same and *are* exactly the same, no matter which person is actually mouthing the words.

Libs Would Have No Work

What would the late-night comics and entertainers do without President Donald J. Trump?

Nothing.

They wouldn't have jobs!

Meanwhile, those of us who are conservatives—including those of us who have chosen to #WalkAway from the Democratic socialists and the liberals and everyone else on the left in order to *live our own lives*, as we see fit, not as they see fit—are celebrating that we're free.

We celebrate that we have walked away from all that hate, shame, blame, and regret.

And we are fighting to be heard.

We are working *for* America, *for* the American people, and *for* ourselves and our beliefs.

We have so many reasons to celebrate our freedom and to fight for it every single day.

And we never forget, ever, all of the brave Americans who have served, bled, died, and given everything so that we can be free and remain free.

Our president wholeheartedly supports them and honors their sacrifices, too. Virtually every day he publicly thanks our nation's servicemen and servicewomen, thanks our military, our police, our firefighters, our first responders, and so many others who serve in some of the toughest professions on this planet today.

Our police are being ripped apart, vilified, criticized, and slammed badly this year. Their budgets are being slashed in major cities across America, even as crime is now rising. (Look at the horrible gun-violence epidemic in New York City right now, in July 2020, as I write these words. Chicago, too, is reeling from gun violence. It's abysmal.)

Bad cops need to get out now. We can all agree on that. But the vast majority of law enforcement are good cops, as I've said before. The vast majority are great people, full of guts, and proud of America.

There is so much good that this president stands for—and he is fighting for us every day.

Yep, we love our president.

We love our country!

NOW, HERE'S MY REAL-LIFE TIP FOR YOU for living as a free American in 2020 and well beyond: Fly the American flag.

Defend our country.

Stick up for it.

It's too easy these days to put down America, to take cheap shots at our beautiful nation, to throw in with the haters against the U.S.A.

Yes, our country has its troubles, its issues, and its challenges.

But our country needs all of us to help make it better than it already is.

It is *still*—and always will be—the greatest country on Earth.

Just don't fall for all the blanket bullcrap that you hear from liberals day and night. Be patriotic for America and proud of all that's good in our country.

Most of all, express your heartfelt beliefs and exercise your responsibility as a free American by voting for Trump in this year's presidential election.

Wherever you are in your own life's journey, I hope you'll have the confidence to find your most passionate calling as a kickass conservative who believes in our country and wants to fight for the best of America, today and always.

And as you do this, take a deep dive into your own potential.

Open up your power and spiritual destiny.

Your future is up to you.

Live as you want to, without hurting anyone else. I'm just laying this out here for you.

Don't let others derail you or mislead you.

Don't buy into the constant negativity on the other side.

We get one chance to make our mark on this earth. So let's live our best life!

Follow your heart.

Follow your dreams.

Be happy.

Be proud of yourself.

One of the greatest assets we have as Americans is the American Dream. It's brought millions upon millions of bright-eyed immigrants to this land with the hopes of achieving something greater than they left behind, and it's still happening now. They hope for a better future for themselves and their family.

It's absolutely delicious and beautiful to dream big. In fact, it's our birthright as spiritual beings.

God didn't create us to stay small. No three-year-old dreams of growing up and doing just "OK" to get by.

That's ludicrous. That is the type of weak, crippling mindset that enables victimhood ("I can't do it because of...").

Actually, yes you can!

We can if we work hard. We *can* if we dream big. And we sure as hell *can* if we believe that we can.

That's the conservative way.

If you're reading all of this and thinking, "But Joy! I don't have time to do this," then you need to wake up.

You don't have time *not* to do this, seriously.

I'm telling you to get out a pen and a piece of paper, go somewhere private, put away your phone, and unleash your imagination *right now*.

This is for you. Jot down quickly what you think your perfect day is. What you would do as soon as you wake up—to what you would do right before you go to bed.

If the stage were set exactly as you want it, what would that look like? What does the "scene" look like?

Who are you married to or partnered with?

Are you surrounded by pets? By antiques? By a team working for you, *with* you?

Maybe it's all of these.

Maybe it's not.

Figure it out. This is *your life*.

How are you going to practice self-mastery to become the strongest, most capable version of yourself as a kickass conservative?

What does true personal freedom mean to you in a workable, day-to-day scene?

Who do you want to become? What do you want to do? What do you want to have?

Ask yourself all of this. Go nuts on this!

Be extravagant. Create the life you've always wanted.

Be in love with your gorgeous and intelligent soulmate.

Be leading the nation in truth.

Be highly favored and blessed by God.

Be the biggest, baddest, coolest version of yourself that you always knew in your heart you desired, yet were told by others, "It's too much."

Who do you want to become? What do you want to do? What do you want to have?

What was your biggest dream before your parents, your bosses, your friends—or your non-friends—told you to chill the f*** out and just "settle"?

Never settle!

One of the biggest things in my own life is my ability to dream big. I've always written down my goals and journaled, knowing that the bigger my vision, the truest to myself and the more organized I must be.

I have an embarrassing number of notebooks scribbled to pieces with my goals, purposes, desires, and over-the-top dreams.

And you know what? If I didn't have those, I know for a fact that I wouldn't be here right now writing this book.

So do this for yourself.

Go ahead! Do it today.

Carve out your own future. It's up to you.

You can do it.

And as a kickass conservative, I'm here to cheer you on!

CHAPTER 9

Everything Else You Always Wanted to Know

My Answers to Your Burning Questions

"Every time you are tempted to react in the same old way, ask if you want to be a prisoner of the past or a pioneer of the future." —Deepak Chopra

I'M VERY ACTIVE ON social media and I get lots of questions from all of my JoyTribe and so many other people—about who I am and what I've done, about being a kickass conservative, about helping our country.

Here is some of what you've asked me recently, along with my answers.

I picked 12 of your most urgent, compelling, interesting questions—from a pool of tons of others!

And I'm always brutally honest.

My goal is to help you, guide you, share resources, and encourage you to live your best life and your truest life. So let's dive right in.

QUESTION #1: Tell us more about yourself, Joy Villa. About you, as a person. You inspire us and we want to know more.

ANSWER: OK, here goes. My ex-husband, Thorsten, to whom I was married for three years (2016-2019) and was with for a total of seven years, wanted me to be his muse, his "manic pixie dream girl." Even though I played that part and sometimes gained from it, I came to the realization that I'm so much more than a cinematic trope as seen through the eyes of a male.

I was destined to pass through—and yes, *change*—his life, to bring spontaneity, color, vibrancy, and wildness. We had a beautiful marriage that I'm forever grateful for; we remain good friends today. But all of that was meant to be traded for self-awareness, growth, and a sense of being grounded.

I have learned practical skills. And yes, I have a yearning for new motherhood!

I am quirky. A bit flighty. But I'm strong, persistent, stubborn.

I have a loud laugh, a raspy voice, big hair, and a wild and amazing taste in fashion and design.

I collect too much stuff, love cats too much, and get addicted easily to changing things.

I crave compliments and cuddles, and I am desperate to make a name for myself.

I'm horrible at numbers and math.

I fart when I laugh.

I lose track of time.

And I complain about things I actually enjoy.

I also become ravenous and rude when I'm hungry, get grumpy when I don't get to work out, and am obsessed with physical health.

Oh, yes, and I love baking vegan chocolate chip cookies and indulging in pizza when I'm craving a treat!

I'm also weirdly political even though I hate politics.

I'm religious, even though I'm a free-spirited spiritualist.

I'm a member of the NRA. I believe in protecting our Second Amendment, not devaluing it. I believe that a well-armed woman is a strong woman.

I've been selfish and can be bratty. I'm working on that!

I've accepted my faults and my many mistakes.

I love fully and deeply. I'm a hopeless romantic.

I need nature, but I am drawn to big cities.

I'm feminine and girly, yet I've chosen the path of most resistance.

I understand that life is not about being perfect. It's about "being." It's about daring to exist even when society, parents, friends, education, or background tells us not to do that.

It's about living dangerously outspoken. It's about saying "no" when something or someone no longer serves us—daring to say "no" without saying we're sorry or making hurried excuses for why something doesn't work.

Just, *"NO!"*

I'm not perfect—and I don't want to be. But I'm f***ing successful and vibrant and loving. *I'm blessed and I know it!*

And when I pray to God, I know that He's going to give me the things I need. If He closes the door, I know He will open a window.

I don't stop until all windows, all doors, all back alleys, and all fences are closed to me. Only then do I know it is not God's will, but I will fight to my last breath to achieve the greatness I know that God has placed on me, the mantle I was meant to achieve, and the crown I was meant to wear.

QUESTION #2: What are your thoughts about Joe Biden as a presidential candidate?

ANSWER: I really don't care about Biden. He's a poor excuse for a political candidate.

I care about getting President Trump reelected in November 2020. He's the leader our country needs to stay strong and to grow even stronger in the future.

Biden has been an elected official for decades, yet he's done nothing for the Black community. He's done nothing for the White community.

He's nothing but a fame-chasing old man who's out of touch with reality. Keepin' it real here, guys. It's how I feel.

Many of you have also asked me about Biden's promise to choose a woman as his vice-presidential running mate—maybe a Black woman, as others are telling him to do. That's sheer identity politics. And he's boxed himself into a corner.

I also think it's an outrage that in May of this year, Biden told Charlamagne tha God on "The Breakfast Club" radio show, "If you have a problem figuring out whether you're for me or Trump, then you ain't Black."

Biden apologized later, but it's still not OK.

That Biden comment would be outrageous if it weren't so—*outrageous.* This guy is—to use a word some of my Jewish friends use now and then—a class-A schmuck. It's true.

Biden doesn't support Black business or Black enterprise. He supports Black people in name only—and he's the one who helped draft that horrible crime bill back in the 1990s, when Bill Clinton was president and which the Democrats supported. The Violent Crime Control and Law Enforcement Act of 1994 hurt Black and brown people—and we're still trying to undo its effects. It led to more prison sentences and more aggressive policing of people of color.

With the First Step Act, President Trump and conservatives in Congress are trying to undo many of the ill effects of that old Biden crime bill. In 2018, Trump signed the First Step Act into law, something I myself advocated for at the White House, along with Kim Kardashian and many others. It's helping inmates return to society successfully as productive individuals by expanding their access to rehabilitative programs.

(You can read more about the First Step Act at www.whitehouse.gov

and search "Trump championed reforms." You'll see a useful fact sheet there.) One other thing that's relevant here. When I voted for the Obama-Biden ticket in the 2008 and 2012 presidential elections, I thought I was doing the right thing. Remember, this was before I truly understood conservatism. This was before I actively, left liberalism behind.

Obama seemed like our generation's Kennedy. He was young, Black, and handsome.

But he turned out to be a letdown in every possible way.

During the Obama-Biden years, more Black Americans were on welfare, and more Black Americans were out of work. Even my own cousins couldn't get work under Obama-Biden.

But now, with Trump as our president and in this incredible Trump economy—which is beginning to roar back after the vicious coronavirus scourge as I write this—they've found work.

This isn't rocket science. Biden is bad for Black people. He's bad for business. He's bad for America.

On top of all of this, Biden is now saying that if he's elected in November, he'll grant U.S. citizenship to 11 million illegal immigrants—plus do a "full erasure" of all of Trump's tough border policies. This is apparently part of the Democrat Party's "new unity platform." Biden would also expand sanctuary locations across the country.

Does anyone really think that this would strengthen our nation? *Are you kidding me?*

When Election Day comes around this November and it's time to cast a vote for president, I think that many swing voters and independents, and even Democrats in name only, will be confused. Why? Because they've "always voted" Democrat, just as my Black and Latin American families did for years.

But I'm here to tell you that a Biden ticket is not the answer to solving

~ 163 ~

America's race-relation issues, America's economic needs, or America's financial independence from foreign oil and foreign governments.

President Trump, on the other hand, has shown for the past four years that he is the right man to lead our country. *He believes in our country 100 percent.* In 2020, 2021, and beyond, I have full confidence that Trump will continue to be a man of his word and show us, the American people, that he values our sovereignty, our independence, and our freedom—just as our Founders did.

The question, "Is it Trump or Biden in November 2020?" is not even a question at all when you consider that radical socialism has hijacked today's Democratic Party. It's ridiculous.

We've seen countless socialist views and comments from leftists like AOC (Rep. Alexandria Ocasio-Cortez of New York) and Omar (Rep. Ilhan Omar of Minnesota). These far leftists are essentially leading the Democratic Party right now. And if by some chance Biden does get in, which I don't believe he will, these radical leftists will pull him even further to the left than he already is and be the ones running our country. That's frightening.

House Speaker Nancy Pelosi of California would do that, too. *Ugh!* (Pelosi, by the way, said in a TV interview at the end of June that a federal mandate to wear face masks in America was "long overdue." See how these Democrats try to swipe at Trump and chip away at our conservative values and personal freedoms every chance they get?)

There's the very creepy aspect of Biden, too, with all the hair sniffing and the getting-too-close-to-young-girls action on his part. And what about the allegations by Lucy Flores, a former Nevada congresswoman, that he assaulted her years ago when she worked in his Senate office? He denied it, but it's not been fully resolved.

Other women have also had issues with his touching, his nose rubbing, and so much else over the years. Biden is just *creepy.* That's my opinion.

QUESTION #3: How do you feel about what President Trump did on the night of June 1 of this year—how he walked from the White House, after making a speech in the Rose Garden, went to St. John's Episcopal Church, and held up a Bible? The mainstream media and even some religious leaders slammed him for it.

ANSWER: Let me give you a very full response.

In June, hundreds if not thousands of looters in many cities bashed storefront windows at night and stole goods and property as our police forces tried to control the mayhem and chaos, as I mentioned earlier in this book. I saw the destruction myself in my own city of Los Angeles.

But by and large, this was not the work of peaceful protesters who were, and still are, angry about the death of George Floyd in Minneapolis. As I noted earlier, Floyd should not have died—and the police responsible for Floyd's untimely death must be brought to justice.

But the thugs, looters, and rioters who ransacked retail outlets across our country—and, worse, physically hurt and even killed people—were not helping anyone. They were hurting America.

Wanton destruction never leads to positive solutions. One police source in New York City said that when the looting was going on in Manhattan and elsewhere, "We're so lucky that whole buildings and blocks did not burn down."

In Los Angeles, I met some of the National Guard who were there because of the riots, as I noted previously. I was at the corner of Hollywood and Highland, which was all boarded up because of the rioting and looting. And when the National Guard heard who I was, some of them wanted a picture with me.

They were on edge at first, but then it was totally chill. We melted their hearts that day.

Here's the truth: I believe in out-creating all the negativity out there in

Joy Villa

I believe completely and wholeheartedly in our country's future!

the world. We're going to be fine. God is good. And President Trump, who is standing up for America, is amazing.

My dad used to say, "God is good, people are great, life is wonderful." He would say that to me all the time. It was his mantra. Now I'm saying it, too, to stay positive and to stay above the fray. And please use it yourself if it helps you.

We're making it through all of this. Trump is going to get reelected absolutely after this, as he's showing so much strength and taking care of our country. When Trump gave that amazing speech in the Rose Garden on June 1, he declared himself the "president of law and order"—which he has always been.

He called the rioting and looting "a total disgrace."

"We cannot allow the righteous cries of peaceful protesters to be drowned out by an angry mob," he said. He blamed professional rioters, anarchists, and extremists like Antifa for the harm and destruction and chaos that's been happening. And he mobilized federal resources to stop that destructive behavior.

Then—surprising almost everyone—the president walked out the front gates of the White House, as you mentioned in your question, and headed across Lafayette Park to St. John's Episcopal Church. Just one night earlier, looters set fire to part of this beautiful church. So its windows were boarded up, and graffiti was everywhere. It looked awful.

Trump, holding a Bible, stood where looters and rioters had been the night before, and reclaimed this turf. To me, it was a stunning, memorable moment.

Yep, as usual, many on the left ripped Trump's actions. As I've mentioned to you before, when was the last time anyone on the left praised our president for *anything*?

And by the way, would any media ever say this about Obama if Obama had walked to the church as Trump had? (You know the answer to that.)

Trump is leading the way on religious freedom in this country. That's part of what happened in D.C. on June 1.

But the liberal media won't tell you that.

And he is doing everything he can to keep our country safe while destructive forces try to rip it apart. Stay focused on Trump 2020!

QUESTION #4: How do I tell my family I'm a conservative?

ANSWER: Ooh, this is big!

The answer comes down to your comfort level. Do you feel comfortable making a big, dramatic announcement about this in a group setting?

For some people, that's the only way to go, as they feel it will clear the air.

If this is your situation and your instinct is to go this route to articulate your beliefs, I say go for it.

I'm behind you all the way.

But you must do what's right for *you.*

Find *your* solution.

We can't control how others will react. But we can live our own lives honestly and with integrity and passion.

If your style is to be quieter and more low-key about your political beliefs, that's fine, too. Some people prefer just taking one parent or sibling aside and sharing how they think, and not making a big deal about it.

A third option is to remain quiet publicly but to privately vote your conscience. I know plenty of people who live this way.

They're fervently pro-Trump, but they can't or won't tell their families or friends, for a ton of reasons! While that's sad to me—it prevents others from knowing and understanding their honest beliefs—I understand it.

The truth is sometimes too painful for others to comprehend.

Two other points I'll share here: Did we ever twist ourselves into a pretzel on a question like this during the Obama years? (*Exactly.*)

And this: Family dynamics change over time as people grow, as different experiences occur. So if you don't see an opportunity right now to articulate your true political beliefs to your family (or don't feel the environment is friendly enough), things might change sooner than you think.

Be patient.

Stick to your guns.

Find others who are likeminded and who share your beliefs.

And wait for your moment.

QUESTION #5: As an Afro-Latina woman, do you feel the protests and riots after George Floyd's death were really about Black Lives Matter—or something else?

ANSWER: Many people were out there with Black Lives Matter signs. And many of them believe that expression—that Black lives do matter—in their hearts.

As I've said, what happened to George Floyd was horribly unfair. It was unjust.

But too many people resorted to violence and decadence—and they're still doing it in some areas of the country as I finish this book.

For these types, it's not about Black Lives Matter. It's not about justice for George Floyd.

For them, it's about controlling the narrative. It's about fear. They want people to be in fear, to live in fear.

My own area, my home neighborhood, had a curfew due to a lot of this. I couldn't leave my home at night.

You probably can't believe that a Black woman is talking like this, by the way. Well, believe it. All Black women do not speak as a monolith.

We are not a monolith. We have our own individual thoughts.

All of this, of course, comes on the heels of COVID-19 and quarantining, when Democrat governors—like Newsom in my home state of California—have been telling us to stay home to save lives, to stay on lockdown. And to *return* to lockdown now.

Yes, we were already in a very stressful situation in this country.

Look at how many lives were destroyed and how many businesses have been destroyed because of these lockdowns. And there have been many cases of domestic violence, of child abuse, because people literally couldn't and can't go anywhere to escape.

So a lot of this is political. A lot of this is to take down Trump.

I believe that 100 percent and I'm calling B.S. when I see it.

I want to give you all some sanity.

I'm here with you. You're not alone.

Most of all, I want people to be safe.

We have had a really tough time this year, but we will get through it and come back even stronger. We must be smart, have a great deal of understanding, and learn from our mistakes.

I know that President Trump feels this way, too, and he's doing all he can. I believe in this country's future, its promise, all of the good here. We can move past this. People need to keep working. They need their jobs. We need our businesses fully open again. We need our economy thriving again.

We can be responsible as individuals in our country and *as* a country.

Trump is the one to keep leading our nation.

QUESTION #6: How'd you get started in the entertainment business?

ANSWER: Thank you for that question. Here's a long answer with probably more detail than you ever expected!

I've been an artist ever since I was a child. At three years old, I drew a picture of a cat on a napkin. My mom saved it, raved about it, and showed it to everyone. It's a story she told the whole family every holiday season!

She said she knew right then that her little girl was going to be an artist.

Even as a kid, I never stopped trying new things. I wrote poetry at a young age, and I thought I would become an illustrator, like my favorite children's book authors, because I loved reading. My mom taught me to read at a very young age before I went to school. And I would get up early every Saturday and Sunday to draw with my dad—one of the pleasures of my young life.

I still think fondly about it as I continue to draw and paint. I started painting with pastels at age eight. I continue to paint and create beautiful artwork today.

But at five years old, when I was in my first play, a Christmas play, the performance bug truly bit. I played an angel in the story of Christ's birth at Maranatha Christian Academy in Orange County, California. My mom created the costume, and I distinctly remember, like it was yesterday, telling her to "make sure it looked right."

Oh, yes, I was a little diva!

I wanted the sash to be perfect. I wanted it to be sparkly and shiny. I wanted my dress to be modern, beautiful, elegant, and flowing. And my crown needed to fit exactly and my wings attached precisely, as if I could really fly!

Belonged on Stage

Early on, I understood the power of performance. I knew as I was singing, performing, and becoming a character that I had to look the part.

Everything came together for me. I loved being on stage—the lights, dressing up, looking beautiful for the audience, feeling beautiful, and playing the part of an angel who was heralding Christ's birth. I knew I belonged on stage.

Fast forward a bit. My parents put me in dance lessons and in gymnastics. I took modern dance and ballet lessons, and at age 10, acting classes. I ended up performing in a local theatre troupe that put on "Fiddler on the Roof" and other great plays. I was part of the chorus. I learned how to work with a team. I learned discipline, my lines, and my dance steps. It was profound for me.

As I continued acting, I knew that my destiny was to be an actress, an artist, a teacher, and a mentor to others through my art.

And I knew that I would be famous! I even thought I'd be a Disney celebrity, a Disney kid, at age 14.

It didn't quite end up like that, but at 15 years old I joined youth programming for a local TV station owned by Comcast. Working in youth network television was one of the best things I ever did.

The program was run by Chris Brock, a tall, super-tanned, white-haired hippie who loved bringing television to kids. He trained children to operate cameras and to run video software under the supervision of adults.

BABY JOY
Joy
I GOT MY START AT 15 HOSTING LIVE TV FOR YOUTH NETWORK TV

There I was, at about 15 years old, hosting a program on Youth Network TV for over 40,000 viewers every Friday on Comcast in Santa Barbara. Those were incredible times, and I look back fondly on them.

They started me on my journey of impacting the culture

through television and media. In my small town of Lompoc, California, I would get recognized on the street. People would say, "Aren't you the girl on TV?"

And I'd chirp back, "Yes!"

In the local newspaper, there was a picture of me, shy but pretty, with the long dreadlocks I wore back then. I knew that I was destined for bigger and even better things, and I couldn't wait to move out of our small town and get back to Manhattan—where we had made regular trips for auditions as a family, and where, in some ways, I actually felt like I had been raised.

I also wanted to live in Los Angeles and become famous and help others—be the next Oprah!

Bit of Personal History

I continued to hone my acting craft, and I continued dancing and doing public speaking as well. As part of the Youth City Council, I helped our town move forward on building a skate park. I was really proud of that, too.

You could say that it was my first foray into politics, which I've had a love-hate relationship with for years. I did love making a difference and speaking in front of adults as a teenager, speaking out against the drugs that seemed to be infesting our city, speaking out against the hopelessness that kids felt because we didn't have a skate park or a better YMCA or some other good outlet for our energy.

Fast forward to now, as a young woman of 34—and art and politics are intertwined in my life in a beautiful marriage of sorts, which I didn't think was possible back then. But it's real.

I always thought my art would be the thing that changed the world and that public speaking might be something on the side.

But neither of them is "on the side." They're each important, each vibrant, each a big part of my life. And it's not over until you stop. As my mom used to say, "It ain't over 'til the fat lady sings"—and she hasn't sung yet! She hasn't even warmed up.

At Lompoc High School, I continued to act in plays, and after my parents moved to Burbank, I left home at age 18 and traveled with my first boyfriend around the country. I came back home and ended up studying in North Hollywood, at the Actors' Boot Camp, taking intensive six-week courses in acting and communications. Then, at Celebrity Centre in Hollywood, I built a strong backbone in acting, which intertwined with my guitar playing.

Finally, in 2011, that's where things began happening with my music, as I noted a little bit earlier in this book. Music is actually the tip of my pyramid. In my career, I do many things, which some people have actually looked down on me for—you know, "she's a jack of all trades, master of none"—which is so ridiculous to even say. My creative endeavors all complement each other.

I act, I sing, I dance, I write. And yes, I've even gotten into directing, producing, and filmmaking, as well as fashion design, makeup artistry, public speaking, and political activism. I have a certification in nutrition, too, and I've worked as a personal trainer. As I shared earlier as well, I've been a bikini bodybuilder, placing third in my first competition.

I always say I don't have hobbies. I make a career out of everything I do!

It goes back to something my mom always said. She said that even in my crib as a baby, I was *busy, busy, busy.*

That's how I'm happiest.

A wise man once said, "Production is the basis of morale."

I believe that.

It's hard for a busy person to be unhappy. So the pyramid, at the tip-

Me with my Auntie Sherill, a warm, loving, and wonderful person in my life.

top, shows the number-one career choice. The rest follow from that, much like the food pyramid.

Around this time, I moved to New York City as an adult and pursued music there. I also modeled and appeared in music videos (I mentioned some of this earlier, too). And since I was an Obama fan at this time, I appeared in an Obama campaign music video and got paid for it.

Even now, some people find that online and try to use it against me, saying things like, "See? She's a fake conservative." (Yep, it's those haters again.)

Thank God for the #WalkAway movement. It demonstrated that you actually *can* leave the liberal mindset behind in the dust once you realize it's all wrong for you—and come over to the good side.

You can come out of the "Empire" and join the "Jedi."

I don't deny my past. It shaped me and brought me here—and it will continue to shape me. I'm proud of all that I've done. But I'm proudest of *my present* because it's going to bring me to *my future*.

I continued to shape myself musically and artistically. I wrote more songs, and "Vagabonds" ended up becoming a No. 1 Billboard hit on my EP, "I Make The Static." The song was about traveling and kicking your heels up, but I wrote it before I ever traveled around the world on tour to 35 countries.

That's the magic of words. *What we put out into the world can attract what we want.*

Now here I am! And you know the other parts of my life, including my new song, "Voice Over Violence" with Ricky Rebel, because I've described them all in this book. (For even more news, go to www.joyvilla.com.)

QUESTION #7: Will you ever run for office?

ANSWER: In late 2017 and early 2018, I set up an exploratory committee for a potential run for Congress. I got thousands of letters of support, and I was able to get to the amount of $5,000 through many, many small donations of just $25 and $50. My thought was that I would run as an outsider—a non-politician who truly wanted to make things better. Trump did that, too, of course. My JoyTribe kept pushing me toward a congressional run, supporting me and urging me on in my dream. I'm so grateful for that.

In the end, I felt that my voice was too wild, too pure, for the really thick, deep swamp—and realized that I truly belong in the arts, in the creative and performing arts scene, which right now for me is in Hollywood. This is where I can make the most change. It's why I'm encouraging other artists to come out strongly as conservatives.

My story shows that you can come from small means and make a gigantic difference. Doesn't matter where you start from. It matters where you end up!

QUESTION #8: What can I do as a young "regular citizen" to help the conservative cause?

ANSWER: Great! You want to contribute? You want to do more?

Here's how. Get educated on conservative values. Get that knowledge. Information—good, solid, reliable information about conservatism and conservatives—is available in many places.

For starters, see the recommended reading I share at the back of this book.

I also advise getting to know the personal success stories of many prominent American conservatives. Learn and read about the paths they took, the lives they've led, and the lives they're leading today. You will improve your sense of control over the whole messy, overwhelming area of politics and pop culture.

Finally, if you want to help local conservatives get elected this fall, reach out to the Republican Party committee in your home state.

Most of the GOP state websites will direct you to local candidates and tell you how you can get involved. The California Republican Party website, for example, has opportunities for volunteering, donating, receiving regular communications, and more.

QUESTION #9: Do you believe in finding a love relationship that's "forever"?

ANSWER: Yes, I do. I believe in finding your soulmate and your one true love. But sometimes it takes loving other people first and realizing that they're not the right ones for you before you find someone you simply can't be without. You're on the same page with this person, and you know your life is different after meeting him or her—and there's no going back.

It's why I say: Don't marry out of convenience. Don't marry because you think society is telling you to get married.

I'm at peace now with what happened with my marriage to Thorsten, which lasted three years, as I noted. And I'm so blessed to be able to be friends with him to this day. He's a very talented photographer and artist.

As of this writing, I'm in a wonderful relationship with a new man, and I'm blessed to be with someone who embraces me even with all my flaws. We laugh together; we make fun of each other. And our relationship isn't based on money, or politics, or grandstanding, or any of those things.

Ryan is my love, and I adore the hell out of him.

He's his own person—strong, intelligent, and willing to work. And one day he wants to have kids and get married as well, so our goals are aligned. While we don't know what our future holds, we're building it and growing together.

I met him in January right before this year's Grammys, and we've been inseparable ever since.

And by the way, I'm writing a dating book.

So stay tuned for that!

QUESTION #10: Tell us about the charity work you do.

ANSWER: Charity work is very important to me! I have raised millions of dollars for some very special charities that deliver much-needed services. I've supported efforts to stop human trafficking and to get people off drugs. My specific focus has been to help kids become drug-free, especially in the United States, where drugs are such a huge problem.

Having had experiences myself with drugs, I know how critical this work is and how much our children need our help. And I've been blessed to have raised over $1 million for the Foundation for a Drug-Free World.

I've also been active in disaster relief. One such charity I'm proud to be an ambassador for is Mercury One. Working alongside Suzanne Grisham, my friend and the CEO of the charity, I was able to help raise over $2 million after the flooding in Texas in 2017. It was an honor for me to be on the ground in that state, to be right there with so many of the people who were impacted, helping to dig through the flooded homes and assist those in desperate circumstances. We gave gift cards to families so that they could buy needed things like food and toilet paper. We delivered diapers and other supplies to churches so that they could distribute those goods.

I even helped prepare the food for a good old Texas barbecue for those who had been displaced. As a vegan, I skipped the meat—but I made some mean veggies.

Another charity that I support, and for which I'm an ambassador, is the Way to Happiness Foundation. It works with the United in Peace Foundation to deliver peace-focused educational materials to rival gangs in the inner cities of Compton and Los Angeles. The charities help elicit conversation as well. This work is so important, as I get to help stop violence in the inner cities of Black America. During the "peace rides," we pray and travel with the grieving mothers of children lost to gang violence.

I've also raised and donated funds for several anti-human trafficking entities in Los Angeles. I consider this one of my greatest accomplishments, too. I'm looking forward to being a billionaire, as our president is, so that I can build schools, educate children, create charities and organizations, and help in the social betterment of our nation.

We don't need to depend on the government to do it. This is how a kickass conservative serves the community.

QUESTION #11: Do you believe in God's will?

ANSWER: God is so good. I am just blown away by that understanding. God is so good that he took a young girl from where I was in the world to where I am now. *It could only be God.*

It's incredible. I opened myself to following His will and to be blessed.

God is always there waiting to help you. He is always there ready to lead you and help you.

He already carved a path out for you.

Now it's up *to you* to walk it.

I'm a preacher's daughter, you know, so don't let me preach now—but I'm going to have to! It's always up to each one of us to use the legs that God gave us—or lose the path.

Use it or lose it. We have to walk that path.

That's why, when people say, "Oh, God didn't want me to get that job," or things like that, I know it is not true. The fact is that God gave you a body and a mind and the intelligence and the means. Of course He wants you to get a job!

The real questions are these: What did you do to help yourself? Did you go out there and apply? Did you submit résumés? Did you knock on doors? Did you make the phone calls?

And did you then make *follow-up* phone calls after all that?

Can't Blame Stuff on God

It takes a great deal of effort to succeed in this world. People tend to forget that, or to pooh-pooh it. A lot of people will blame God when they don't succeed. Or they'll say that God doesn't want them to succeed, or that God must not have wanted certain things for them.

I have a problem with people saying that when they're talking about something they obviously need to do on their own, in order to survive or to take care of their family.

For example, it is *not* God's will that you don't pay your child support just because you "don't have the money this month."

You can't say that! That is not God's will.

But it *is* God's will that you get off your ass, put the Cheetos down, stop watching the porn, and go out there and provide for your kids—who completely *depend on you and need you.* It's a problem when people use God as an excuse for not doing what they need to do as parents. And if you give up because you're afraid, or because your family says you shouldn't do something, or because you think God doesn't want something for *you*—well, it truly could be you who's *stopping yourself* in your own journey.

Many times, we say that something in our lives is "the devil at work." But many times, the devil takes on the face in the mirror. We really don't need the devil to stop us when we do all that negative work ourselves!

We think that we're not pretty enough, not strong enough, not handsome enough, not good-looking enough, not rich enough, not polite enough, not educated enough to do all the things we want to do. Yet all of these things are *excuses.*

The hard-boiled truth is that each of us is enough, just as we are.

You are enough. And you have always been enough. And you will always be *enough* to achieve greatness. You just have to believe it and go after it and do it in the only way you know how, in a way that is uniquely yours.

And when I say these things to you—my JoyTribe and all my readers and followers—I'm also saying these things to myself.

QUESTION #12: What did you think of President Trump's major event at Mount Rushmore on the eve of July 4?

ANSWER: Amazing. Patriotic. Bold. Brave. Inspiring.

I am proud to be an American. I love this country so much. I'm proud of our Constitution, our flag, and our nation of patriots.

I'm also sick and tired of liberals thinking that they're winning the culture wars in this country. And no one should *ever* apologize to the leftist mob.

I'm very proud of our president. President Trump must be reelected this November and he *will* be reelected in November 2020. We need him to continue making us stronger than ever.

And as I told Aubrey Huff on his podcast, *Off the Cuff*, for a special July 4th program this year (shortly before my book went to press), our president was elected fairly. He's been running our country in an amazing way—and he helped bring us the best economy before COVID. And now it keeps climbing back.

Even during this crisis, he's handled it impeccably, in my opinion.

This is a man who just doesn't take any B.S.

He wants to give power back to the people.

Here's part of what Trump said at Mount Rushmore: "There could be no better place to celebrate America's independence than beneath this magnificent, incredible, majestic mountain and monument to the greatest Americans who have ever lived."

"Today, we pay tribute to the exceptional lives and extraordinary legacies of George Washington, Thomas Jefferson, Abraham Lincoln, and Teddy Roosevelt," he also said. "I am here as your president to proclaim before the country and before the world: This monument will never be desecrated—these heroes will never be defaced, their legacy will never, ever be destroyed, their achievements will never be forgotten, and Mount Rushmore will stand forever as an eternal tribute to our forefathers and to our freedom."

His Executive Order

The president also said this, a little later on in his speech: "Under the executive order I signed last week—pertaining to the Veterans' Memorial Preservation and Recognition Act and other laws—people who damage or deface federal statues or monuments will get a minimum of 10 years in prison. And obviously, that includes our beautiful Mount Rushmore."

"Our people have a great memory," Trump added. "They will never forget the destruction of statues and monuments to George Washington, Abraham Lincoln, Ulysses S. Grant, abolitionists, and many others."

"The violent mayhem we have seen in the streets of cities that are run by liberal Democrats, in every case, is the predictable result of years of extreme indoctrination and bias in education, journalism, and other cultural institutions."

He continued, "Against every law of society and nature, our children are taught in school to hate their own country, and to believe that the men and women who built it were not heroes, but that they were villains. The radical view of American history is a web of lies—all perspective is removed, every virtue is obscured, every motive is twisted, every fact is distorted, and every flaw is magnified until the history is purged and the record is disfigured beyond all recognition."

Trump also said, "This movement is openly attacking the legacies of every person on Mount Rushmore. They defile the memory of Washington, Jefferson, Lincoln, and Roosevelt. Today, we will set history and history's record straight."

"Before these figures were immortalized in stone, they were American giants in full flesh and blood, gallant men whose intrepid deeds unleashed the greatest leap of human advancement the world has ever known."

Trump, of course, said much more in his extraordinary speech—and was frequently interrupted by applause.

Check out these additional comments by the president!

"We believe in equal opportunity, equal justice, and equal treatment for citizens of every race, background, religion, and creed. Every child, of every color—born and unborn—is made in the holy image of God."

"We want free and open debate, not speech codes and cancel culture. We embrace tolerance, not prejudice," said Trump.

"We support the courageous men and women of law enforcement. We will never abolish our police or our great Second Amendment, which gives us the right to keep and bear arms."

"We believe that our children should be taught to love their country, honor our history, and respect our great American flag."

(You can read the entire Trump speech from the Mount Rushmore event at www.whitehouse.gov and search "Mount Rushmore speech.")

All of this and more is why I'm fighting for our country and will fight for it until the day I die.

It's why I back Trump 100 percent.

And this is why, as kickass conservatives, we're going to reelect President Donald J. Trump in November 2020!

CHAPTER 10

. . . .

Feedback from the Fans (My JoyTribe)

Yes, Your Voice Really Does Matter

*"Think twice before you speak, because your words
and influence will plant the seed of either success or failure
in the mind of another." —Napoleon Hill*

ERE'S A SELECT SAMPLING of some of the uplifting, intriguing, thoughtful, and motivating comments that you've all shared with me recently.

Thank you to each and every one of you, for all you do to share your energy and your passion and to become the most incredible *kickass conservatives* you can possibly be—and to help our country!

I read all of your comments. (I may not always respond right away! But I do read what you write.)

I see them during my live video chats and YouTube events.

I see your messages, your thoughts, your questions, and your observations on virtually all social media.

I appreciate it all! Many others do, too.

I value it all.

I learn from it and grow from all of it.

Your voices are valuable.

Your thoughts count.

Your actions on behalf of our country speak even louder!

I'm nourished by your positivity and by your engagement, and I know that everyone reading this book and reading your comments will be, too.

And I hope and pray that I nourish all of you on a regular basis *and in this book, especially.*

Maybe you'll see your own comments in this collection here.

Either way, I encourage you to keep speaking out and to keep sharing your opinions. Please keep sending me your thoughts, reactions, and reflections.

Keep speaking out on behalf of President Donald J. Trump.

We need everyone in this battle.

Your words inspire all of us to keep speaking out on behalf of our great nation and on behalf of kickass conservatives everywhere!

I know each you will inspire many others as well.

* * *

"I believe in what you represent as a person. It's not about politics or saying the right thing. It's that you are true to yourself and living for the greater good of life and in faith."

"Beauty, strength, a voice that both calms and exhilarates, and an unyielding personality [are] a combination that inspires others to achieve their own dreams and aspirations."

"Villa is amazing and brave … Let's win this fight for our country."

"We need more creative spirit and positive energy like this for our side."

I am living my life with integrity, passion, and courage. You can, too!

"You go where you want and keep telling the truth. It burns them up [the liberals] to see such a stunning woman break free of their tentacles."

"I'm getting very fatigued by the anti-Trump message that is constantly being pushed in the media, and it is great to see someone like Joy Villa take a brave stand against the tide."

"Finally an artist and musician who is smart enough 2 think 4 herself."

"Go, Joy! Thank you *always* for FIGHTING THE GOOD FIGHT!"

"Liberals' worst enemy: a Black conservative because they can't use the race card."

"You have a beautiful aura. God's light shines through you. Keep praying. I am praying for you. Love you, Joy."

"Thanks for standing up for freedom. I know in your business it's not easy to do. You're being true to yourself. Without that, we have nothing. God bless!"

"Joy, you are amazing, and this country and the world [are] going through hard times. God has the answers before we are born. All bad things turn good and better at the other end. Promise and believe. Trump!"

"I'm a MAGA supporter. I choose to just stay quiet almost 100 percent of the time, and come election time, [I will] vote for [whichever candidate] will stay the course of placing America and her citizens first."

"Joy has been fighting for Trump and his supporters from the *beginning!* We see you! We love you!"

"Total respect for you, Miss Joy Villa. Talented, courageous, classy, and honest."

"Love prevails. America: united we stand, divided we fall. Learn tolerance. Learn to love one another. It can be achieved."

"Never stop speaking truth."

"I admire your courage and how you're proud to be a Trump supporter, just as I am."

"I love Joy! I love positive! 'I don't wanna live in the darkness; I want to step into the light. I can't stand the darkness, seeping into my soul.' God, I love that lyric! What reason could anyone ever have for threatening Joy Villa?"

"As a Black American, [I feel] we must start holding ourselves accountable. We must do it now, because one day our time will end. We will stand in front of the Lord God Almighty and we will all be judged, no matter what color."

"I love you, Joy. So glad to have good female influences representing us."

"Don't worry: Once Biden hits the debates, his campaign will be dead."

"Support the country you live in, or live in the country you support."

"Joy, you love America, and Americans love you back. God bless you."

"Fake news is the enemy of the people. Love Trump 2020."

"We need more people who speak their mind like you, Joy. To me, you were the start of the trend of people not being scared to come out and support POTUS."

"Thank you for reminding us that we can be proud of who we are."

"She literally brings *joy* to my soul."

"Trump 2020!"

RECOMMENDED READING LIST
FOR CONSERVATIVES

Check these out.

Educate yourself and stay in the know.

I mentioned some of these books and websites earlier in these pages.

I'm mentioning others here for the first time, and I want you to know about them.

My overall advice: Stay positive.

Acquire knowledge.

Read, listen, and learn.

And take inspiration from others to be your most informed and influential kickass conservative!

And make sure to vote for Trump in the November 2020 election.

BOOKS ·

United States of Socialism: Who's Behind It. Why It's Evil. How to Stop It
by Dinesh D'Souza

Unplanned: The Dramatic True Story of a Former Planned Parenthood Leader's Eye-Opening Journey Across the Life Line by Abby Johnson

The Seven Guaranteed Steps to Spiritual, Family and Financial Success
by Jesse Lee Peterson

The MAGA Doctrine: The Only Ideas That Will Win the Future
by Charlie Kirk

Ship of Fools: How a Selfish Ruling Class Is Bringing America to the Brink of Revolution by Tucker Carlson

Triggered: How the Left Thrives on Hate and Wants to Silence Us
by Donald Trump Jr.

Hard Times Create Strong Men: Why the World Craves Leadership and How You Can Step Up to Fill the Need by Stefan Aarnio

The 10 Laws of Enduring Success by Maria Bartiromo with Catherine Whitney

Raising a Strong Daughter in a Toxic Culture: 11 Steps to Keep Her Happy, Healthy, and Safe by Meg Meeker, M.D.

Dianetics: The Modern Science of Mental Health by L. Ron Hubbard

Men Are from Mars, Women Are from Venus by John Gray, Ph.D.

Women Who Work: Rewriting the Rules for Success by Ivanka Trump

America Return to God: Repent from Sin, Rebuild the Wall, Repair the Gates, Restore the Dream by Alveda C. King

The Right Side of History: How Reason and Moral Purpose Made the West Great by Ben Shapiro

Busting the Barricades: What I Saw at the Populist Revolt by Laura Ingraham

Understanding Trump by Newt Gingrich, foreword by Eric Trump

Live Free or Die: America (and the World) on the Brink by Sean Hannity

Campus Battlefield: How Conservatives Can WIN the Battle on Campus and Why It Matters by Charlie Kirk, foreword by Donald Trump Jr.

There Goes My Social Life: From Clueless to Conservative by Stacey Dash

American Crusade: Our Fight to Stay Free by Pete Hegseth

The Case for Trump by Victor Davis Hanson

The Know Your Bill of Rights Book: Don't Lose Your Constitutional Rights, Learn Them! by Sean Patrick

The 5 Love Languages: The Secret to Love that Lasts by Gary Chapman

The 7 Habits of Highly Effective People by Stephen R. Covey

How to Win Friends and Influence People by Dale Carnegie

Why I Couldn't Stay Silent by David J. Harris Jr.

WEBSITES AND RESOURCES

www.joyvilla.com

www.donaldjtrump.com

www.gop.com

www.foxnews.com

www.oann.com

www.dailywire.com

www.newsmax.com

www.waynedupree.com

www.theepochtimes.com

www.walkawaycampaign.com

www.conservative.org

https://cpac.conservative.org

www.tpusa.com

https://trumpstudents.org

www.dineshdsouza.com

www.larryelder.com

https://bonginoreport.com

www.anncoulter.com

www.hannity.com

www.alvedaking.com

www.politicon.com

www.whitehouse.gov

www.ffcoalition.com

www.abbyjohnson.org

https://savethestorks.com

www.sba-list.org

www.lifesitenews.com

www.nrlc.org

www.liveaction.org

www.focusonthefamily.com

www.thewaytohappiness.org

www.unitedinpeace.org

www.foxbusiness.com/shows/mornings-with-maria

https://thefallenstate.tv

https://aubreyhuff.com/podcasts-off-the-cuff

www.scottbaio.com

https://davidharrisjr.store

https://rickyrebelrocks.com

https://deplorablechoir.com

https://piratadellastrada.com

https://lexitmovement.org

www.infowars.com

www.aa.org

https://mercuryone.org

ACKNOWLEDGMENTS
TO KICKASS PEOPLE

I want to thank: Ryan. Your help, laughs, and tenderness have uplifted me and aided me on my path to becoming a better woman. I love you!

I also want to thank: My brother Ryjin, Auntie Sherill, Uncle Joe, and my amazing cousins Randi, Babie, China, and Baby Jaxon. Also: Jon and Jo Alex Statham, my wonderful assistant "A.J.," my photographer Matthew Cali, my phenomenal editor-collaborator Maureen Mackey (I couldn't have created this without you!), the ever-tireless Brandon Straka, Isaiah Washington, my soul sisters Jacqueline van Bierk and Elizabeth G'Sell, Amanda and Aaron Greene, "Dark" Mark White, Ivanka Trump, Lara Trump, Carolyne Neuman Liberty and Max Liberty, Alex and Mara Edwards, Megan Kashat, the Gunzel Family, Kerri Kasem, Ana and Ted McGrath, Eric M., Jenni F., Pastors Ché and Sue Ahn of Hrock Christian Church, Celebrity Centre Hollywood, the Jewish Republican Alliance, Maria Bartiromo, Tucker Carlson, Sean Hannity, Laura Ingraham, Ben Shapiro, Roger Stone, Ann Coulter, Suzanne Grisham, my awesome formatter Laurie Szostak, and John "Nacho" David Castillo.

And anyone else I forgot! I still love you (don't be mad).

Even though I may not get to see you as often as I like, I truly love and admire each of you!

You have all had a hand in shaping my incredible journey toward today and the future, and I'm excited to share this universe with you!

PHOTOGRAPH CREDITS

Cover designs by Laurie Szostak

Front cover photo © Matt Cali Photography;
styling by Melissa Currie-White

Front cover background by Itana © 123RF.com;
back cover photo by Freepik.com

Inside photos are provided courtesy of the author, except for
the following: pages 3, 5, 31, 36, 41, 69, 75, 105, 111, 133, 138,
145, 166, 187 © Thorsten von Overgaard

Page 14 and Joy Villa author page: © Matt Cali Photography

ABOUT JOY VILLA

Joy Villa is a pro-life, pro-America, pro-Second Amendment conservative singer and actress in Hollywood who loves the Trump administration and has been outspoken as a regular political commentator on *Fox & Friends*, *Mornings with Maria*, *Hannity*, *Watters' World*, and many other programs.

She is regularly at the White House and was appointed to the Trump campaign advisory board in 2017 by Senior Adviser Lara Trump.

Following her appearance at the 2017 Grammys in her "Make America Great Again" Trump dress, her EP, "I Make The Static," rocketed to the No. 1 spot on both iTunes and Amazon. She beat out Beyoncé, Adele, and Lady Gaga, and her album landed at No. 1 in Alternative, No. 1 in Rock, and No. 12 on Billboard's Top 200 Albums.

She has toured in over 35 countries as a performer and now lives in Los Angeles with her cats, her guitar, and her boyfriend.

Her newest song is "Voice Over Violence," featuring Ricky Rebel.

She is active on social media, and her YouTube page has garnered millions of views; she speaks directly and frequently to her fans and followers there.

Learn more about Joy at www.joyvilla.com.

CPSIA information can be obtained
at www.ICGtesting.com
Printed in the USA
BVHW041155250820
587259BV00010B/355